TOM SLADE WITH THE COLORS

PERCY K. FITZHUGH

1st WORLD
LIBRARY
Literary Society

Tom Slade with the Colors

Percy K. Fitzhugh

© 1st World Library, 2007
PO Box 2211
Fairfield, IA 52556
www.1stworldlibrary.com
First Edition

LCCN: 2007934226

Softcover ISBN: 978-1-4218-9670-0
Hardcover ISBN: 978-1-4218-9770-7
eBook ISBN: 978-1-4218-9570-3

Purchase *"Tom Slade with the Colors"*
as a traditional bound book at:
www.1stWorldLibrary.com/purchase.asp?ISBN=978-1-4218-9670-0

1st World Library is a literary, educational organization
dedicated to:

- Creating a free internet library of downloadable ebooks

- Hosting writing competitions and offering book publishing
scholarships.

Interested in more 1st World Library books? contact:
literacy@1stworldlibrary.com
Check us out at: www.1stworldlibrary.com

1ˢᵗ World Library Literary Society

Giving Back to the World

"If you want to work on the core problem, it's early school literacy."

- James Barksdale, former CEO of Netscape

"No skill is more crucial to the future of a child, or to a democratic and prosperous society, than literacy."

- Los Angeles Times

"Literacy... means far more than learning how to read and write... The aim is to transmit... knowledge and promote social participation."

- UNESCO

"Literacy is not a luxury, it is a right and a responsibility. If our world is to meet the challenges of the twenty-first century we must harness the energy and creativity of all our citizens."

- President Bill Clinton

"Parents should be encouraged to read to their children, and teachers should be equipped with all available techniques for teaching literacy, so the varying needs and capacities of individual kids can be taken into account."

- Hugh Mackay

TABLE OF CONTENTS

CHAPTER I

TOM MAKES A PROMISE

Tom Slade hoisted up his trousers, tightened his belt, and lounged against the railing outside the troop room, listening dutifully but rather sullenly to his scoutmaster.

"All I want you to do, Tom," said Mr. Ellsworth, "is to have a little patience—just a little patience."

"A little tiny one—about as big as Pee-wee," added Roy.

"A little bigger than that, I'm afraid," laughed Mr. Ellsworth, glancing at Pee-wee, who was adjusting his belt axe preparatory to beginning his perilous journey homeward through the wilds of Main Street.

"Just a little patience," repeated the scoutmaster, rapping Tom pleasantly on the shoulder.

"Don't be like the day nursery," put in Roy. "All their trouble is caused by having very little *patients*."

"Very bright," said Mr. Ellsworth.

"Eighteen candle power," retorted Roy. "I ought to have

ground glass to dim the glare, hey?"

The special scout meeting, called to make final preparations for the momentous morrow, had just closed; the other scouts had gone off to their several homes, and these three—Tom Slade, Roy Blakeley and Walter Harris (alias Pee-wee)—were lingering on the sidewalk outside the troop room for a few parting words with "our beloved scoutmaster," as Roy facetiously called Mr. Ellsworth.

As they talked, the light in the windows disappeared, for "Dinky," the church sexton, was in a hurry to get around to Matty's stationery store to complete his humdrum but patriotic duty of throwing up a wooden railing to keep the throng in line in the morning.

"The screw driver is mightier than the sword, hey, Dink?" called the irrepressible Roy, as Dinky hurried away into the darkness.

"All I wanted to say, Tom," said Mr. Ellsworth soberly, "is just this: let me do your thinking for you—even your patriotic thinking—for the time being. Do you get me? Don't run off and do anything foolish."

"Is it foolish to fight for your country?" asked Tom doggedly.

"It might be," retorted the scoutmaster, nothing daunted.

"I'm not going to stay here and see people drowned by submarines," muttered Tom.

"You won't see them drowned by submarines as long as you stay here, Tomasso," said Roy mischievously. He loved to make game of Tom's clumsy speech.

Percy K. Fitzhugh

"You know what I mean," said Tom; "I ain't going to be a slacker for anybody."

"You might as well say that President Wilson is a slacker because he doesn't go off and enlist in some regiment," said Mr. Ellsworth; "or that Papa Joffre is a coward because he doesn't waste his time with a rifle in the trenches."

"Gee whiz, you can't say *he's* a coward," exclaimed Pee-wee, "because I saw him!"

"Of course, that proves he isn't a coward," said Roy slyly.

"There's going to be work, and a whole lot of it, for every one to do, Tom," continued Mr. Ellsworth pleasantly. "There is going to be work for old men and young men, for women and girls and boys—and scouts. And being a slacker consists in not doing the work which you ought to do. If a girl has a flower bed where she might grow tomatoes, and she grows roses there instead, you might call *her* a slacker.

"The officials in Washington who have this tremendous burden on their shoulders have told us what *we*, as scouts (Mr. Ellsworth always called himself a scout), ought to do. They have outlined a program for us. Now if you run off and join the army in the hope of doing a man's work, why then some man has got to knuckle down and do your work. See?"

"I'm sick of boring holes in sticks," grunted Tom.

"Well, I dare say you are. I never said it was as pleasant as eating ice cream. What I say is that we must all knuckle down and do what we can do best to help defend Old Glory. And we can't always choose our work for ourselves. I'm going to stay here, for the present, at least, and keep you scouts busy. And I don't consider that I'm a slacker either. If you all stand by me and help, I can be of more service right here, just now, than I could be if I went away."

"Then why does the government have posters out all around, urging fellers to join the army?" said Tom, unconvinced.

"There are fellers and fellers," said Mr. Ellsworth, mimicking Tom's pronunciation of the word, "and what is best for one isn't necessarily best for another. These posters are for fellows older than you, as you know perfectly well. I'm talking now of what is best for *you*—at present. Won't you trust me? If you can't obey and trust your scoutmaster, you couldn't obey and trust your captain and your general."

"I never said I didn't," said Tom.

"Well, then, leave it to me. When the time comes for you to join the army, I'll tell you so, and I'll shout it so loud that you can't make any mistake. Meanwhile, put aside all that idea and knuckle down and help. You're just as much with the colors now as if you were in the trenches.... You'll be on hand early to-morrow?"

"I s'pose so," said Tom sullenly.

Mr. Ellsworth looked at him steadily. No doubt it was something in Tom's grudging manner that made him apprehensive, but perhaps too as he looked at the boy who had been growing up before his eyes in the past two years, he realized as he had not realized before that Tom had come to be a pretty fine specimen and could stand unconcerned, as he certainly would, at the most rigid and exacting physical test.

When Tom's rapid growth had brought the inevitable advent of long trousers, arousing the unholy mirth of Roy Blakeley and others, Mr. Ellsworth had experienced a jarring realization that the process had begun whereby his scouts would soon begin slipping away from him.

He had compromised with Time by making Tom a sort of assistant scoutmaster and encouraging Connie Bennett to work into Tom's place as leader of the Elk Patrol; and he had lived in continual dread lest Tom (who might be counted on for anything) discover his own size, as it were, and get the notion in his stubborn head that he was too big to be a scout at all.

But Tom had thought too much of the troop and of the Elks for that, and a new cause of apprehension for Mr. Ellsworth had arisen which now showed in every line of his face as he looked at Tom.

"I want you to promise me, Tom, that you won't try to enlist without my permission. If you'll say that and obey Rule Seven the same as you have always obeyed it, I'll be satisfied."

"How about Rule Ten?" said Tom, in his usual dogged, half-hearted manner; "a scout has got to be brave, he's got to face danger, he's—"

"You notice Rule Seven comes before Rule Ten," snapped Mr. Ellsworth. "They put them in the order of their importance. The men who made the Handbook knew what they were about. The question is just whether you're going to continue to respect Rule Seven, that's all."

Mr. Ellsworth knew how to handle Tom.

"Yes, I am," Tom said reluctantly.

"Then that's all there is to it. Give me your hand, Tom."

Tom put out his hand, and as the scoutmaster shook it his manner relaxed into the usual off-hand way which the scouts so liked and which had made him so popular among them.

"President Wilson wasn't in any great rush about going to war, and I don't want you to be in a hurry to get into a uniform. You're in a uniform already, if it comes to that. And the Secretary of War says our little old scout khaki is going to make itself felt. I'd be the last to preach slacking, and when it's time, if the time comes, I'll tell you.... You know, Tom," he added ruefully, "you're getting to be such a fine, strapping fellow that it makes me afraid you'd get away with it if you tried. I don't like to see you so big, Tom—"

"Don't you care," said Pee-wee soothingly, "I'm small still."

"If you were old enough, I wouldn't say anything against it," Mr. Ellsworth added. "But you're not, Tom. Some people don't seem to think there's anything wrong in a boy's lying about his age to get into the army. But I do, and I think you do—Don't you?" he added anxiously.

"Y-e-es."

"Of course, you couldn't enlist without Mr. Temple's consent, he being your guardian, unless you lied—and I know you wouldn't do that."

"You didn't catch me in many, did you?"

"I never caught you in *any*, Tom."

"Well, then—"

"Well, then," concluded Mr. Ellsworth, "I guess we'd all better go home and get some sleep. We've got one strenuous day to-morrow."

"It's going to be a peach," said Roy, looking up at the stars. As they started to move away, Mr. Ellsworth instinctively extended his hand to Tom again.

"I have your promise, then?" said he.

"Y-e-s."

"I'm not stuck on that 'yes.'"

"Yes," said Tom, more briskly.

"That you won't do anything along that line till you consult me?"

"Don't do anything till you count ten," said Roy.

"Make it ten thousand," said Mr. Ellsworth.

"And after you've counted ten," put in Pee-wee, "if you decide to go, I'll go with you, by crinkums!"

"Go-o-d-night!" laughed Roy. "That ought to be enough to keep you at home, Tomasso!"

Tom smiled, half grudgingly, as he turned and started toward home.

"You don't think he'd really enlist, do you?" queried Roy, as he and Pee-wee and Mr. Ellsworth sauntered up the street.

"He won't now," said the scoutmaster. "I have his promise."

"Otherwise, do you think he would?"

"I think it extremely likely."

"And lie about his age?"

Mr. Ellsworth screwed his face into a funny, puzzled look. "There's a good deal of that kind of thing going on," he said, "and I sometimes think the recruiting people wink at it, or perhaps they are just a little too ready to judge by physical appearance. Look how Billy Wade got through."

"He doesn't look eighteen," said Roy.

"Of course he doesn't. But he told them he was 'going on nineteen,' and so he was—just the same as Pee-wee is going on fifty."

Roy laughed.

"The honor of enlisting, the willingness to sacrifice one's life, seems to cover a multitude of sins in the eyes of some people," said the scoutmaster. "Heroic duty done for one's country will wipe out a lot of faults.—It's hard to get a line on Tom's thoughts. He asked me the other day what I thought about the saying, *To do a great right, do a little wrong.* I don't know where he rooted it out, but it gave me a shudder when he asked me."

"He was standing in front of the recruiting station down at the postoffice yesterday," said Roy, "staring at the posters. Goodness only knows what he was thinking about. He came along with me when he saw me."

"Hmmm," said Mr. Ellsworth thoughtfully.

"But I guess he wouldn't try anything like that here—the town is too small," said Roy. "Even the recruiting fellow knows him."

"Yes; but what worries me," said Mr. Ellsworth, "is when he goes to the city and stands around listening to the orators and watches the young fellows surging into the recruiting places. That phrase, *Your country needs you*, is dinging in his ears."

"He'd get through in a walk," said Roy.

"That's just the trouble," Mr. Ellsworth mused. "Tom would never do anything that he thought wrong," he added, after a pause; "but he has a way of doping things out for himself, and sometimes he asks queer questions."

"Well, he promised you, anyway," said Roy finally.

"Oh, yes, that settles it," Mr. Ellsworth said. "All's well that ends well."

"We should worry," said Roy, in his usual light-hearted manner.

"That's just what I *shan't* do," the scoutmaster answered.

"All right, so long, see you later," Roy called, as he started up Blakeley's hill.

Mr. Ellsworth and Pee-wee waved him goodnight. Presently Pee-wee deserted and went down, scout pace, through Main Street, laboriously hoisting his belt axe up with every other step. It was very heavy and a great nuisance to his favorite gait, but he had worn it regularly to scout meeting ever since war had been declared.

CHAPTER II

"BULL HEAD" AND "BUTTER FINGERS"

The lateness of the hour did not incline Tom to hurry on his journey homeward. He was thoroughly discouraged and dissatisfied with himself, and it pleased his mood to amble along kicking a stone in front of him until he lost it in the darkness. Without this vent to his distemper he became still more sullen. It would have been better if he had hunted up the stone and gone on kicking it. But now he was angry at the stone too. He was angry at everybody and everything.

Ever since war had been declared Tom had worked with the troop, doing his bit under Mr. Ellsworth's supervision, and everything he had done he had done wrong—in his own estimation.

The Red Cross bandages which he had rolled had had to be rolled over again. The seeds which he had planted had not come up, because he had buried them instead of planting them. Roy's onion plants were peeping coyly forth in the troop's patriotic garden; Doc Carson's lettuce was showing the proper spirit; a little regiment of humble radishes was mobilizing under the loving care of Connie Bennett, and Pee-wee's tomatoes were bold with flaunting blossoms. A bashful cucumber which basked unobtrusively in the wetness of the ice-box outlet under the shed at Artie Van Arlen's home was growing apace. But not a sign was there of Tom's beans or peas or beets—nothing in his little allotted patch but a lonely plantain which he had carefully nursed until Pee-wee had told him the bitter truth—that this child of his heart was nothing but a vulgar weed.

It is true that Roy Blakeley had tried to comfort Tom by telling him that if his seeds did not come up in Bridgeboro they might come up in China, for they were as near to one place as the other! Tom had not been comforted.

His most notable failure, however, had come this very week when three hundred formidable hickory sticks had been received by the Home Defense League and turned over to the Scouts to have holes bored through them for the leather thongs.

There had been a special scout meeting for this work; every scout had come equipped with a gimlet, and there was such a boring seance as had never been known before. Roy had said it was a great bore. As fast as the holes were bored, Pee-wee had tied the strips of leather through them, and the whole job had been finished in the one evening.

Tom had broken his gimlet and three extra ones which fortunately some one had brought. The hickory had proven as stubborn as he was himself—which is saying a great deal.

He had tried boring from each side so that the holes would meet in the middle; but the holes never met. When he had bored all the way through from one side, he had either broken the gimlet or the hole had come slantingways and the gimlet had come out, like a woodchuck in his burrow, where it had least been expected to appear.

And now, to cap the climax, he was to stand outside one of the registration places the next day and pin little flags on the young men as they came out after registering. The other members of the troop were to be distributed all through the county for this purpose (wherever there was no local scout troop), and each scout, or group of scouts, would sally heroically forth in the morning armed with a shoebox full of these honorable mementoes, made by the girls of Bridgeboro.

And meanwhile, thought Tom, the Germans were sinking our ships and dropping bombs on hospitals and hitting below the belt, generally. He was not at all satisfied with himself, or with his trifling, ineffective part in the great war. He felt that he had made a bungle of everything so far, and his mind turned contemptuously from these inglorious duties in which he had been engaged to the more heroic role of the real soldier.

Perhaps his long trousers had had something to do with his dissatisfaction; in any event, they made his bungling seem the more ridiculous. His fellow scouts had called him "bull head" and "butter fingers," but only in good humor and because they loved to jolly him; for in plain fact they all knew and admitted that Tom Slade, former hoodlum, was the best all-round scout that ever raised his hand and promised to do his duty to God and Country and to obey the Scout Law.

The fact was that Tom was clumsy and rough—perhaps a little uncouth—and he could do big things but not little things.

As he ambled along the dark street, nursing his disgruntled mood, he came to Rockwood Place and turned into it, though it did not afford him the shortest way home. But in his sullen mood one street was as good as another, and Rockwood

Place had that fascination for him which wealth and luxury always had for poor Tom.

Three years before, when Tom Slade, hoodlum, had been deserted by his wretched, drunken father and left a waif in Bridgeboro, Mr. Ellsworth had taken him in hand, Roy had become his friend, and John Temple, president of the Bridgeboro Bank, noticing his amazing reformation, had become interested in him and in the Boy Scouts as well.

It had proven a fine thing for Tom and for the Scouts. Mr. Temple had endowed a large scout camp in the Catskills, which had become a vacation spot for troops from far and near, and which, during the two past summers, had been the scene of many lively adventures for the Bridgeboro boys.

But Tom had to thank Temple Camp and its benevolent founder for something more than health and recreation and good times. When the troop had returned from that delightful woodland community in the preceding autumn and Tom had reached the dignity of long trousers, the question of what he should do weighed somewhat heavily on Mr. Ellsworth's mind, for Tom was through school and it was necessary that he be established in some sort of home and in some form of work which would enable him to pay his way.

Perhaps Tom's own realization of this had its part in inclining him to go off to war. In any event, Mr. Ellsworth's perplexities, and to some extent his anxieties, had come to an end when Mr. Temple had announced that Temple Camp was to have a city office and a paid manager for the conduct of its affairs, which had theretofore been looked after by himself and the several trustees and, to some extent, by Jeb Rushmore, former scout and plainsman, who made his home at the camp and was called its manager.

Whether Jeb had fulfilled all the routine requirements may be a question, but he was the spirit of the camp, the idol of every boy who visited it, and it was altogether fitting that he should be relieved of the prosy duties of record-keeping which were now to be relegated to the little office in Mr. Temple's big bank building in Bridgeboro.

So it was arranged that Tom should work as a sort of assistant to Mr. Burton in the Temple Camp office and, like Jeb Rushmore, if he fell short in some ways (he couldn't *touch* a piece of carbon paper without getting his fingers smeared) he more than made up in others, for he knew the camp thoroughly, he could describe the accommodations of every cabin, and tell you every by-path for miles around, and his knowledge of the place showed in every letter that went out over Mr. Burton's name.

From the window, high up on the ninth floor, Tom could look down behind the big granite bank building upon a narrow, muddy place with barrel staves for a sidewalk and tenements with conspicuous fire escapes, and washes hanging on the disorderly roofs. This was Barrel Alley, where Tom had lived and where his poor, weary mother had died. He could pick out the very tenement. Strangely enough, this spot of squalor and unhappy memories held a certain place in his affection even now.

Tom and Mr. Burton and Miss Ellison, the stenographer, were the only occupants of the little office, but Mr. Temple usually came upstairs from the bank each day to confer with Mr. Burton for half an hour or so.

There was also another visitor who was in the habit of coming upstairs from the bank and spending many half hours lolling about and chatting. This was Roscoe Bent, a young fellow who was assistant something-or-other in the bank and whose fashionable attire and worldly wisdom caused Tom to stand in great awe of him.

Roscoe made no secret of the fact that he came up in order to smoke cigarettes, which practice was forbidden down in the bank. He would come up, smoke a cigarette, chat a while, and then go down again. He seemed to know by inspiration when Mr. Burton and Mr. Temple were going to be there. Up to the morning of this very day he had never shown very much interest in either Tom or Temple Camp, though he appeared to entertain a lively interest in Miss Ellison, and Tom envied him his easy manner and his faculty for entertaining her and making her laugh.

On the morning of this day, however, when he had come up for his clandestine smoke, he had manifested much curiosity about the camp, looking over the maps and pictures and asking many questions.

Tom had felt highly flattered.

CHAPTER III

ROSCOE BENT

Indeed, Tom had felt so highly flattered that the memory of young Mr. Roscoe Bent's condescension had lingered with him all day, and now he was going to give himself the pleasure of walking through Rockwood Place for a passing glimpse of the beautiful house wherein young Roscoe resided.

Tom knew well enough that Roscoe had to thank the friendship between his father and Mr. Temple for his position in the bank. In his heart he knew that there was not much to be said for Roscoe; that *he* could do many things which Roscoe couldn't begin to do; but Roscoe on the other hand could do all those little things which poor Tom never could master; he could joke and make people laugh, and he always knew what to say and how to say it—especially to girls.

Tom's long trousers had not brought him this accomplishment, and in his clumsiness of speech and manner he envied this sprightly youth who had become so much of a celebrity in his thoughts that he actually took a certain pleasure in walking past the Bent residence just because it was where Roscoe and his well-to-do parents lived.

Percy K. Fitzhugh

He was a little ashamed of doing this, just as he was ashamed of his admiration for Roscoe, and he knew that neither Roscoe, with his fine airs, nor Roscoe's home would have had any attractions for Roy at all. But then Roy's father was rich, whereas Tom's father had been poor, and he had come out of the slums and in some ways he would never change.

"He isn't so bad, anyway," Tom muttered to himself, as he kicked another stone along. "I knew he'd be really interested some day. Any feller's *got* to be interested in a camp like that. If he only *went* there once, he'd see what it was like and he'd fall for it, all right. I bet in the summer he goes to places where they dance and bow, and all that, but he'd fall for Temple Camp if he ever went there—he would."

Tom was greatly elated at Roscoe's sudden interest, and he believed that great things would come of it.

"If he could only once see that shack up on the mountain," he said to himself, "and make that climb, I bet he'd knock off his cigarettes. If he thought those pictures were good—gee, what would he think of the shack itself!"

When he reached the Bent house he was surprised to see an automobile standing directly in front of it which he had not noticed as he approached because its lights were out. Not even the little red light which should have illuminated the car's number was visible, nor was there a single light either in the entrance hall or in any of the windows of the big house.

In the car sat a dark figure in the chauffeur's place, and Tom, as he passed, fancied that this person turned away from him. He was rather surprised, and perhaps a little curious, for he knew that the Bents did not keep a car, and he thought that if the presence of the machine meant visitors, or a doctor, there would be some light in the house.

Reaching the corner, he looked back just in time to see another figure, carrying luggage, descend the steps and enter the car. He was still close enough to know that not a word was spoken nor a sound made; there was not even the familiar and usual bang of the automobile door. But a certain characteristic swing of the person with the luggage, as he passed one bag and then the other into the car, showed Tom that the figure was that of young Roscoe Bent. Then the car rolled away, leaving him gaping and speculating in the concealment of a doorway near the corner.

"I wonder where he can be going this time of night," Tom mused. "Gee, that was funny! If he was going on a vacation or anything like that, he'd have said so this morning—and he'd have said good-bye to me. Anyway, he'd have said good-bye to Miss Ellison...."

Tom boarded with a private family in Culver Street, and after he reached home he sat up in his room for a while working with a kind of sullen resignation on the few registration badges which had still to have pins attached to them.

It was while he was engaged in this heroic labor that a thought entered his mind which he put away from him, but which kept recurring again and again, and which ended by cheating him out of his night's sleep. Why should Roscoe Bent be leaving home with two suitcases at twelve o'clock at night when he would have to register for the selective draft the next day?

After this rather puzzling question had entered his mind and refused to be ousted or explained away, other puzzling questions began to follow it. Why had the lights of the automobile been out? Why had there been no lights in the house?

Why had no one come out on the porch to bid Roscoe good-bye? Why had not Roscoe slammed the auto door shut, as one naturally did, that being the easiest way to shut it?

Well, all that was Roscoe's business, not his, thought Tom, as he settled down to go to sleep, and perhaps he had closed the door quietly because he wished not to disturb any one so late at night. That was very thoughtful of Roscoe....

But just the same Tom could not go to sleep, and he lay in bed thinking uneasily.

He had just about conquered his misgivings and had begun to think how suspicious and ungenerous he was, when another question occurred to him which had the effect of a knockout blow to his peace of mind.

Why had Roscoe Bent told Miss Ellison that it was better to be a live coward than a dead hero?

—Why, he had only been joking, of course, when he said that! It was one of those silly, careless things that he was always saying. Miss Ellison had not seemed to think it was very funny, but that had only made Roscoe laugh the more. "I'd rather kill time than kill Germans," he had said lightly. And Miss Ellison had said, "You're quite brave at killing time, aren't you?"

It was just joking and jollying, thought Tom, as he turned over for the fourth or fifth time, and he wished that *he* could joke and jolly like that. He made up his mind that when Roscoe came upstairs in the morning he would ask him whether the Germans weren't cowards to murder innocent women and children, and whether he would really want to be like them. He believed he could say that much without a tremor, even in front of Miss Ellison.

He wished morning would come so that he could be sure that Roscoe ... so that he could say that when Roscoe came upstairs.

"I'll bet he'll be sleepy after being out so late," thought Tom.

CHAPTER IV

THE CUP OF JOY

Tom was to have the next day off for his patriotic activities, but he went to the Temple Camp office early in the morning to get the mail opened and attend to one or two routine duties.

He found Miss Ellison already at her desk, and she greeted him with a mysterious smile.

"I hear you're going to be one of the celebrities," she said, busying herself with her typewriter machine.

"One of the what?" said Tom.

"One of the leading figures of the day. I don't suppose you'll even *look* at poor me to-morrow.—I was down in the bank and Mr. Temple said to send you down as soon as you came in."

"Me?" stammered Tom.

"Yes, you."

For a few seconds Tom waited, not knowing what to say or

do—especially with his feet.

"You didn't notice if Roscoe was down there, did you?" he finally ventured.

"I most certainly did not," answered Miss Ellison, smiling with that same mysterious smile, as she tidied up her desk. "I have something else to think of besides Mr. Roscoe Bent."

Tom shifted from one foot to the other. "I thought you— maybe—kind of—I thought you liked him," said he.

"Oh, did you?"

He had never been quite so close to Miss Ellison before, nor engaged in such familiar discourse with her. He hesitated, moving uneasily, then made a bold plunge.

"I think you can—I think a person—I think a feller can tell if a girl kind of likes a certain feller—sort of—"

"Indeed!" she laughed. "Well, then, perhaps you can tell if I like *you*—sort of."

This was too much for Tom. He wrestled for a moment with his embarrassment, but he was in for it now, and he was not going to back out.

"I'm too clumsy for girls," said he; "they always notice that."

"You seem to know all about them," said the girl; "suppose I should tell you that *I* never noticed any such thing.—A girl usually notices if a fellow is strong, though," she added.

"It was being a scout that made me strong."

"There are different ways of being strong," observed Miss Ellison, busying herself the while.

"I know what you mean," said Tom. "I got a good muscle."

She leaned back in her chair and looked at him frankly. "I didn't mean exactly that," she said. "I meant if you make up your mind to do a thing, you'll do it."

Again Tom waited, not knowing what to say. He felt strangely happy, yet very uncomfortable. At length, for lack of anything better to say, he observed:

"I guess you kinder like Roscoe, all right."

For answer she bent over her typewriter and began to make an erasure.

"Don't you?" he persisted, gaining courage.

"Do I have to tell *you*?" she asked, laughing merrily.

Tom lingered for a few moments. He wanted to stay longer. This little familiar chat was a bigger innovation in his life than the long trousers had been. His heart was pounding just as it had pounded when he first took the scout oath. Evidently the girl meant to leave early herself, and see something of the day's festivities, for she was very prettily attired. Perhaps this, perhaps the balmy fragrance of that wonderful spring day which Providence had ordered for the registration of Uncle Sam's young manhood, perhaps the feeling that some good news awaited him down in Mr. Temple's office, or perhaps all three things contributed to give Tom a feeling of buoyancy.

"Are you going to see the parade?" he asked. "I got a badge

here maybe you'd like to wear. I can get another for myself."

"I would like very much to wear it," she said, taking the little patriotic emblem which he removed from his khaki coat. "Thank you."

Tom almost hoped she would suggest that he pin it on for her. He stood for a few moments longer and then, as he could think of nothing more to say, moved rather awkwardly toward the door.

"You look splendid to-day, Tom," Miss Ellison said. "You look like a real soldier in your khaki."

"The woman where I board pressed it for me yesterday," he said, blushing.

"It looks very nice."

Tom went down in the elevator, and when it stopped rather suddenly at the ground floor it gave him exactly the same feeling that he had experienced while he talked to Miss Ellison....

Roscoe Bent was not at his desk as he passed the teller's window and glanced through it, but he did not think much of that, for it was early in the day and the sprightly Roscoe might be in any one of a dozen places thereabout. He might be up in the Temple Camp office, even.

John Temple, founder of Temple Camp and president of the bank, sat at his sumptuous desk in his sumptuous office and motioned Tom to one of the big leather chairs, the luxuriousness of which disconcerted him almost as much as had Miss Ellison's friendliness.

"I told Margaret to send you down as soon as you came in, Tom," said Mr. Temple, as he opened his mail. "I want to get this matter off my mind before I forget it. You know that General Merrill is going to be here to-night, I suppose?"

"I heard the committee was trying to get him."

"Well, they've got him, and the governor's going to be here, too; did you hear that?"

"No, sir, I didn't," said Tom, surprised.

"I've just got word from his secretary that he can spend an hour in our little berg and say a few words at the meeting to-night. Now listen carefully, my boy, for I've only a few minutes to talk to you. This thing necessitates some eleventh-hour preparation. The plan is to have a member from every local organization in town to form a committee to receive the governor and the general. That's about all there is to it.

"There's the Board of Trade, and the Community Council, and—let's see—the churches and the Home Defense and the Red Cross and the Daughters of Liberty and the Citizens' Club, and the Boy Scouts."

Already Tom felt flattered.

"Each of these organizations has designated one of its members to act on the committee. I had Mr. Ellsworth on the phone this morning and told him he'd have to represent the scouts. He said he'd do no such thing—that he wasn't a boy scout."

"He's the best scout of all of us," said Tom.

"*He* says you're the best," retorted Mr. Temple; "so there you are."

"Roy's got twice as many merit badges as I have," said Tom.

"Well, you've got long trousers, anyway," said Mr. Temple, "and Mr. Ellsworth says you're the representative scout, so I guess you're in for it."

"*M-me?*"

"Now, pay attention. You're to knock off work at the registration places at five o'clock and go up to the Community Council rooms, where you'll meet these ladies and gentlemen who are to form the reception committee. Reverend Doctor Wade will be looking for you, and he'll take you in hand and tell you just what to do. There won't be much. I think the idea is to meet the governor and the general with automobiles and escort them up to the Lyceum. The committee'll sit on the platform, I suppose. Doctor Wade will probably do all the talking.... You're not timid about it, are you?" he added, looking up and smiling.

"Kind of, but—"

"Oh, nonsense; you just do what the others do. Here—here's a reception committee badge for you to wear. This is one of the burdens of being a public character, Tom," he added slyly. "Mr. Ellsworth's right, no doubt; if the scouts are to be represented at all they should be represented by a scout. Don't be nervous; just do as the others do, and you'll get away with it all right. Now run along. I suppose I'll be on the platform too, so I'll see you there.... You look pretty nifty," he added pleasantly, as Tom took the ribbon badge.

"Mrs. Culver pressed it for me," said Tom. "It had a stain,

Percy K. Fitzhugh

but she got it off with gasoline."

"Good for her."

"Would—do you think it would be all right to wear my Gold Cross?"

"You bet!" said Mr. Temple, busy with his mail. "If I had the scouts' Gold Cross for life-saving, I'd wear it, and I'd have an electric light next to it, like the tail light on an automobile to show the license number."

Tom laughed. He found it easy to laugh. He was nervous, almost to the point of panic, but his heart was dancing with joy.

"All right, my boy," laughed Mr. Temple. "Go along now, and good luck to you."

As Tom went out of Mr. Temple's office he seemed to move on wings. He was half frightened, but happy as he had never been in all his life. His cup of joy was overflowing. He had been through the ordeal of more than one generous ovation from his comrades in the troop; he had stood awkward and stolid with that characteristic frown of his while receiving the precious Gold Cross which this night he would wear.

But this was different—oh, so different! He, Tom Slade, was to help receive the governor of the state and one of Uncle Sam's famous generals. The Boy Scouts were to be represented because the Boy Scouts had to be reckoned with on these occasions, and he, Tom Slade, organizer of the Elk Patrol and now assistant to the scoutmaster, was chosen for this honor.

"I'm glad I had my suit pressed," he thought.

What a day it had been for him so far! He had had a little chat with Margaret Ellison, she had said she liked him—anyway, she had almost said it, and she had taken the little emblem from him and had said that *if he made up his mind to do a thing he would do it*. He remembered the very words. Then he had gone downstairs and received this over-whelming news from Mr. Temple. What if he *had* planted his seeds wrong and bored holes slantingways instead of straight? He was so proud and happy now that he added the official, patented scout smile to his sumptuous regalia and smiled all over his face.

He was usually rather timid about speaking to the men in the bank unless they spoke to him first, for the bank was an awesome place to him; but to-day he was not afraid, and his recollection of the pleasant little chat upstairs reminded him of a fine thing to do.

"Is Rossie Bent here?" he asked, stopping at the teller's cage.

"Bent!" called the teller.

Tom waited in suspense.

"Not here," called a voice from somewhere beyond.

"Not here," repeated the teller, and added: "Asleep at the switch, I dare say."

Evidently the people of the bank had Roscoe's number. A strange feeling came over Tom which chilled his elation and troubled him. Irresistibly there rose in his mind a picture of a waiting automobile, of a dark figure, and a silent departure late at night.

"I guess maybe he's just stopped to register, hey?" said Tom.

"Stopped for something or other, evidently," said the teller.

"Could I speak to Mr. Temple's secretary?" Tom asked.

Mr. Temple's secretary, a brisk little man, came out, greeting Tom pleasantly.

"Congratulations," said he.

"I meant to ask Mr. Temple if I could have a couple of reserved seat tickets for the patriotic meeting to-night," said Tom, "but I was kind of flustered and forgot about it. I could get them later, I guess, but if you have any here I'd like to get a couple now because I want to give them to some one."

"Yes, sir," said the secretary, in genial acquiescence; "just a minute."

Tom went up in the elevator holding the two tickets in his hand. If his joy was darkened by any growing shadow of apprehension, he put the unpleasant thought away from him. He was too generous to harbor it; yet a feeling of uneasiness beset him.

As he entered the office, Margaret Ellison, smiled broadly.

"You knew what it was?" he said boldly.

"Certainly I knew, and isn't it splendid!'

"I got two tickets," said Tom, "for reserved seats down front. They're in the third row. I was going to give them to Roscoe and tell him to take—to ask you to go. But he's—he's late—I guess he stopped to register. So I'll give them to you, and when he comes up you can tell him about it."

"I'll give them to him and say you asked me to."

"All right," Tom said hesitatingly; "then he'll ask you."

"Perhaps."

She disappeared into the little inner office where Mr. Burton was waiting to dictate his mail, and Tom strolled over to the big window which overlooked Barrel Alley and gazed down upon that familiar, sordid place.

It was a long road from that squalid tenement down there to a place on the committee which was to receive the governor of the state. Over there to the left, next to Barrey's junk shop, was poor Ching Wo's laundry, into which Tom had hurled muddy barrel staves. And that brick house with the broken window was where "Slats" Corbett, former lieutenant of Tom's gang, had lived.

A big lump came up in his throat as he thought over the whole business now and of where the scout trail had brought him. Oh, he was happy!

The bright spring sunshine which poured in through the window on that wonderful morning, the flags which waved gayly here and there, seemed to reflect his own joy, and he was overwhelmed with the sense of triumph.

"That was a good trail I hit, all right," he said to himself. He could not have said it out loud without his voice breaking.

One thing he wished in those few minutes of exultation. He wished that his mother might be there to see him on the stage, a conspicuous part of that patriotic demonstration, with the Gold Cross of the scouts upon his left breast. That would make the cup of joy overflow.

But since that could not be, the next best thing would be the knowledge that Margaret Ellison would be sitting there in the third row, looking ever so pretty, and would see him, and notice the Gold Cross and wonder what it meant.

"I'm glad I never wore it to the office," he mused.

And Roscoe Bent, with all his sprightly manners and fine airs, would see where this good scout trail, which he had ridiculed, had brought Tom.

"It's a bully—old—trail—it is," he said to himself; "it's one good old trail, all right."

He took out his handkerchief and rubbed his eyes. Perhaps the bright sunlight was too strong for them.

CHAPTER V

THE MAIN TRAIL

But a trail is a funny thing. It is full of surprises and hard to follow. For one thing, you can never tell just where it is going to bring you out. There is the main trail and there are branch trails, and it is often puzzling to determine which is the main trail and which the branch.

Yet you must determine this somehow, for the one may lead you to food and shelter, to triumph and honor perhaps; while the other, which may be ever so clear and inviting, will lead you into bog and mire; so you have to be careful.

Of one thing you may be certain: there are not often two trails to the same place. You must pick one branch or the other. You must know where you want to go, and then hit the right trail. You must not be fooled by a side trail just because it happens to be broad and easy and pleasant. There are ways of telling which is the right trail, and you must learn those ways; otherwise you are not a good scout.

Upon the sleeve of Tom Slade's khaki jacket was seen the profile of an Indian. It was the scouts' merit badge for pathfinding. It meant that he knew every trail and byway for miles about Temple Camp. It meant that he had picked his

Percy K. Fitzhugh

way where there was no trail, through a dense and tangled wilderness; that he had found his way by night to a deserted hunting shack on the summit of a lonely wooded mountain in the neighborhood of Temple Camp and that he had later blazed a trail to that isolated spot.

Even Rossie Bent had opened his eyes at Tom's simple, unboastful narrative of this exploit, and had followed Tom's finger on the office map as he traced that blazed trail from the wood's edge near the camp up through the forest and along the brook to the very summit of the frowning height, from which the nickering lights of Temple Camp could be seen in the distance.

"I'll bet not many people go up there," Roscoe had said.

So it was natural that when Tom looked back and thought of his career as a scout, of his rise from squalor and vicious mischief to this level of manliness and deserved honor, he should think of it as a trail—a good scout trail which he had picked up and followed. Down there in the mud of Barrel Alley it had begun, and see where it had led! To the platform of the Bridgeboro Lyceum where he, Tom Slade, would wear his Gold Cross, which every citizen at that patriotic Registration Day celebration might see, and would represent the First Bridgeboro Troop, B. S. A. in the town's welcome to the governor!

Oh, he was happy!

"It's good I didn't listen to Slats Corbett and Sweet Caporal," he mused. "I hit the right trail, all right. I bet if—"

The door opened suddenly, and Mr. Brown from the bank entered with another gentleman, who appeared greatly disturbed.

"Has Rossie Bent been up here to-day?" Mr. Brown asked.

"No, sir," said Tom. He felt his own voice tremble a little, and he realized that something was wrong.

"This is Mr. Bent," said Mr. Brown, "Roscoe's father. Roscoe hasn't been seen since last night, and his father is rather concerned about him."

"You haven't seen him—to-day?" Mr. Bent asked anxiously.

"No, sir," said Tom.

The two men looked soberly at each other, and Tom went over to the door of the private office, which stood ajar, and quietly closed it.

"Mr. Burton is busy," he said.

"We might ask him," Mr. Brown suggested.

For the space of a few seconds Tom stood uneasily trying to muster the courage to speak.

"It—it wouldn't be any good to let a lot of people know," he said hesitatingly, but looking straight at Roscoe's father. "Mr. Burton only got here a few minutes ago, and he couldn't tell anything.—If you spoke to him, Miss Ellison would know about it too."

He spoke with great difficulty and not without a tremor in his voice, but his meaning reached the troubled father, who nodded as if he understood.

"It's early yet," Tom ventured; "maybe he'll think it over, kind of, and—and—"

Percy K. Fitzhugh

"Thank you, my boy," said Mr. Bent soberly.

The two men stood a moment, as if not knowing what to do next. Then they left, and Tom remained standing just where he was. Of course, he was not surprised, only shocked.

"I knew it all the time," he said to himself, "only I wouldn't admit it."

He had been too generous to face the ugly fact. To him, who wished to go to war, the very thought of slacking and cowardice seemed preposterous—impossible.

"I was just kidding myself," he said, with his usual blunt honesty, but with a wistful note of disappointment. "There's no use trying to kid yourself—there ain't."

Mr. Burton came out with his usual smiling briskness and greeted Tom pleasantly. "Congratulations, Tommy," said he. "I suppose I'll see you among the big guns to-night. You leaving soon?"

"Y-yes, sir, in a few minutes."

"Miss Ellison and I are so unpatriotic that we're going to work till the parade begins this afternoon."

"I don't suppose he'll even *notice* us to-morrow," teased the girl, "he'll be so proud."

Tom smiled uncomfortably and wandered over to the window where, but a few minutes before, he had looked out with such pride and happiness. He did not feel very happy now.

Close by him was a table on which were strewn photographs

of Temple Camp and the adjacent lake, a few birch bark ornaments, carved canes, and other specimens of handiwork which scouts had made there. There was also a large portfolio with plans of the cabins and pavilion and rough charts and diagrams of the locality.

Tom had shown this portfolio to many callers—scoutmasters and parents of scouts—who had come to make inquiries about the woodland community. He had shown it to Roscoe Bent only the day before and, as we know, he had been greatly pleased at the lively interest which that worldly young gentleman had shown.

He opened the portfolio idly now, and as he did so his gaze fell upon the map which showed the wooded hill and the position of the lonesome shack upon its summit. He called to mind with what pride he had traced his own blazed path up through the forest and how Roscoe had followed him, plying him with questions.

Then, suddenly, like a bolt out of the sky, there flashed into Tom's mind a suspicion which, but for his generous, unsuspecting nature, he might have had before. Was *that* why Roscoe Bent had been so interested in the little hunting shack on the mountain? Was *that* why he had asked if any one ever went up there; why he had inquired if there were fish to be caught in the brook and game to be hunted in the neighborhood? Was that why he had been so particular about the blazed path, and whether there was a fireplace in or near the shack? Had he been thinking of it as a safe refuge, a place of concealment for a person who had shirked his duty?

"He could never live there," said Tom; "he could never even *get* there."

As the certainty grew in his mind, he was a little chagrined at his own credibility, but he was more ashamed for Roscoe.

"I might have known," he said, "that he wasn't really interested in camping.... He's a fool to think he can do that."

To Tom, who longed to go to war and who was deterred only by his promise to Mr. Ellsworth, the extremity that Roscoe had evidently gone to in the effort to escape service seemed unbelievable. But that was his game, and Tom saw the whole thing now as plain as day. It made him almost sick to think of it. While he, Tom, would be handing badges to the throng of proud and lucky young men just fresh from registering, while he sat upon the platform and listened to the music and the speeches in their honor, Roscoe Bent would be tracing his lonely way up that distant mountain with the insane notion of camping there. He would try to cheat the government and disgrace his family.

"I don't see how he could do that—I don't," said Tom. "I wonder what his father would say if he knew.—I wonder what Miss Ellison would say. I wonder what his mother would think."

He looked down again into Barrel Alley, and fixed his eyes upon the tenement where he and his poor mother and his wretched father had lived. But he was not thinking of his mother now—he was thinking of Roscoe Bent's mother and of his troubled father, going from place to place and searching in vain for his fugitive son.

"If I told him," thought Tom, "it would queer Roscoe. It wouldn't do for anybody to know.... I just got to go and bring him back.... Maybe they'd let him register to-morrow. He could say—he could say anything he wanted to about why he was away on the fifth of June. If he comes back they'll let him register, but if he doesn't they'll find him: they'll put his name in newspapers and lists and they'll find him. I just got to go and bring him back. And I got to go without telling anybody anything, too."

For a few moments longer he stood gazing out of the window down into that muddy alley where the good scout trail to honor and achievement had begun for him. For a few moments he thought of where it had brought him and of the joy and fulfillment which awaited him this very night. He wondered what people would say if he were not there. Well, in any event, they would not call him a slacker or a coward. He felt that there was no danger of being misjudged if he did his highest duty.

"It's kind of like a branch trail I got to follow," he said, his voice breaking a little. "I said it was a good trail, but now I see there's a branch trail that goes off, kind of, and I got to follow that...."

But, of course, it wasn't a branch trail at all—it was the main trail, the true scout trail, which, forgetting all else, he was resolved to follow.

Percy K. Fitzhugh

CHAPTER VI

TOM AND THE GOLD CROSS

Mr. Ellsworth was right when he said that Tom had a way of doping things out for himself. He had picked up scouting without much help, and he seldom asked advice.

His duty was very clear to him now. As long as no one but himself and Roscoe knew about this miserable business, the mistake could be mended and no harm come of it.

The thing was so important that the smaller evil of neglecting his allotted task and foregoing the honors which awaited him did not press upon him at all. He was disappointed, of course, but he acknowledged no obligation to anybody now except to Roscoe Bent and those whom his disgrace would affect. Wrong or right, that is the way Tom's mind worked.

Quietly he took his hat and went out, softly closing the door behind him. For a second or two he waited in the hall. He could still hear the muffled sound of the typewriter machine in the office.

As he went down in the elevator he heard two gentlemen talking about the celebration that evening and about the governor's coming. Tom listened wistfully to their conversation.

He had already taken from his pocket (what he always carried as his heart's dearest treasure) a dilapidated bank book. He intended to draw ten dollars from his savings account, which would be enough to get him to Catskill Landing, the nearest railroad point to camp, and to pay the return fare for himself and Roscoe.

But the bank was closed and Tom was confronted by a large placard in the big glass doors:

CLOSED IN HONOR OF OUR BOYS.
DON'T FORGET THE PATRIOTIC RALLY TO-NIGHT.
DO YOUR BIT!
YOU CAN CHEER IF YOU CAN'T REGISTER.

He had forgotten that the bank was to close early. Besides spoiling his plan, it reminded him that the town was turning out in gala fashion, and his thoughts turned again to the celebration in the evening.

"I gotta keep in the right trail," he said doggedly, as he turned toward home.

He did not know what to do now, for he had less than a dollar in his pocket, and he was stubbornly resolved to take no one into his confidence. If he had the money, he could catch a train before noontime and reach the mountain by the middle of the afternoon. He would make a short cut from the railroad and not go up through Leeds or to Temple Camp at all.

As he walked along he noticed that the street was gay with

Percy K. Fitzhugh

bunting. In almost every shop window was a placard similar to the one in the bank. A large banner suspended across the street read:

DON'T FORGET THE RALLY
IN HONOR OF OUR BOYS
TO-NIGHT!

"I ain't likely to forget it," he muttered.

He wondered how Roscoe's father felt when he saw that banner and this thought strengthened his determination so that he ignored the patriotic reminders all about him, and plodded stolidly along, his square face set in a kind of sullen frown.

"It's being—with the Colors, just the same," he said, "only in another kind of way—sort of."

As he turned into West Street he noticed on the big bulletin board outside the Methodist Church the words:

THE GOVERNOR WILL BE ON THE PLATFORM
OUR BOYS WILL BE IN THE TRENCHES
THE BOY SCOUTS ARE ON THE JOB
AND DON'T YOU FORGET IT!

"They're a live bunch, that Methodist Troop, all right," commented Tom.

He raised his hand and gently lifted aside a great flag which hung so low over the sidewalk that he could not walk under it without stooping.

"Just the same, I can say I'm with the Colors," he repeated. "You can be with them even if—even if they ain't around—"

He had evidently hit on some plan, for he walked briskly now through Culver Street, his lips set tight, making his big mouth seem bigger still.

He entered the house quietly and went up to the little room which he occupied. It was very small, with a single iron bed, a chair, a walnut bureau, and a little table whereon lay his Scout Manual and the few books which he owned. Outside the window, on its pine stick, hung a stiff muslin flag which he had bought.

He unlocked the top bureau drawer and took out a tin lock-box. This box was his pride, and whenever he took it out he felt like a millionaire. He had gazed at it in the window of a stationery store for many weeks and then, one Saturday, he had gone in and bought it for a dollar and a half.

He sat on the edge of his bed now, with the box on his knees, and rummaged among its contents. There was the pocket flashlight his patrol had given him; there was the scout jack-knife which had been a present from Roy's sister; an Indian arrow-head that Jeb Rushmore had found; a memorandum of the birthday of his patrol, and the birthdays of its members, and a clipping from a local paper describing how Tom Slade had saved a scout's life at Temple Camp and won the Gold Cross.

From the bottom of this treasure chest he lifted out a plush box which he rubbed on his knee to get the dust off, and then opened it slowly, carefully. He never tired of doing this.

As he lifted the cover the sunlight poured down out of the blue, cloudless sky of that perfect day, streaming cheerily into the plain little room which was all the home Tom had, and fell upon the glittering medal, making it shine with a dazzling brightness.

Percy K. Fitzhugh

Often when Tom read of the Iron Cross being awarded to a submarine commander, or a German spy, or a Zeppelin captain for some unspeakable deed, he would come home and look at his own precious Gold Cross of the Scouts and think what it meant—heroism, *real* heroism; bravery untainted; courage without any brutal motive; the courage that saves, not destroys.

He breathed upon the rich gold now (though it needed no polishing) and rubbed it with his handkerchief. Then he sat looking at it long and steadily. There, shining under his eyes, was the familiar design, the three-pointed sign of the scouts, with the American eagle superimposed upon it, as if Uncle Sam and the scouts were in close partnership.

Tom remembered that the Handbook, in describing the scout sign, referred to it as neither an arrow-head nor a fleur-de-lis, though resembling both, but as a modified form of the sign of the north on the mariner's compass.

"Maybe it's like a fleur-de-lis, so as to remind us of France, kind of," Tom said, as he rubbed the medal again, "and—"

Suddenly a thought flashed into his mind. "And it's pointing to the north, too! It's the compass sign of the north, and it tells me where to go, 'cause Temple Camp and that hill are north from here.... Gee, that's funny, when you come to think of it, how that Gold Cross can kind of remind you—of everything.... Now I know I *got* to do it.... Nobody could tell me what I ought to do, 'cause the Gold Cross has told me.... And it'll help me to ... it will...."

CHAPTER VII

THE TRAIL RUNS THROUGH A PESTILENT PLACE

If Tom had entertained any lingering misgivings as to his path of duty, he cast them from him now. If he had harbored any doubts as to his success, he banished them. Uncle Sam, poor bleeding, gallant France, and the voice of the scout, had all spoken to him out of the face of the wonderful Gold Cross, and he wanted no better authority than this for something which he must do in order to be off on his errand.

Cheerfully removing his holiday regalia, he donned a faded and mended khaki suit and a pair of worn trousers, and as he did so he gave a little rueful chuckle at the thought of poor Roscoe struggling with the tangled thicket in a regular suit of clothes and without any of the facilities that a scout would be sure to take.

He slipped on an old coat, into the pocket of which he put his flashlight, some matches in an airtight box, his scout knife and a little bottle of antiseptic. Thus equipped, he felt natural and at home, and he looked as if he meant business.

Putting the plush box into his pocket, he descended the stairs quietly and slipped into the street. He hurried now, for he wished to get into the city in time to catch the noon train for Catskill.

At the end of Culver Street he turned into Williams Avenue and hurried along through its din and turmoil, and past its tawdry shops until he came to one which he had not seen in many a day. The sight of its dirty window, filled with a disorderly assortment of familiar articles, took him back to the old life in Barrel Alley and the days when his good-for-nothing father had sent him down here with odds and ends of clothing to be turned into money for supper or breakfast.

It spoke well for the self-respect which Tom had gained that he walked past this place several times before he could muster the courage to enter. When he did enter, the old familiar, musty smell and the sordid litter of the shelves renewed his unhappy memories.

"I have to get some money," he said, laying the plush case on the counter. "I have to get five dollars."

He knew from rueful experience that one can seldom get as much as he wants in such a place, and five dollars would at least get him to his destination. Surely, he thought, Roscoe would have some money.

There were a few seconds of dreadful suspense while the man took the precious Gold Cross over to the window and scrutinized it.

"Three," he said, coming back to the counter.

"I *got* to have five," said Tom.

The man shook his head. "Three," he repeated.

"I got to have five," Tom insisted. "I'm going to get it

back soon."

The man hesitated, and looked at him keenly. "All right, five," he said reluctantly.

Tom's hand almost trembled as he emerged into the bright sunlight, thrusting the ticket into a pocket which he seldom used. He had not examined it, and he did not wish to read it or be reminded of it. He felt ashamed, almost degraded; but he was satisfied that he had done the right thing.

"I thought that trail made a bee-line for the platform in the Lyceum," he said to himself, as he folded his five-dollar bill. "Gee, it's a funny thing; you never know where it's going to take you!"

And you never know who or what is going to cross your trail, either, for scarcely had he descended the steps of that stuffy den when whom should he see staring at him from directly across the street but Worry Benson and Will McAdam, of the other local scout troop.

They were evidently bent on some patriotic duty when they paused in surprise at seeing him, for they had with them a big flag pole and several bundles which looked as if they might contain printed matter.

Tom thought that perhaps these were a rush order of programs for the patriotic rally, and he wondered if they might possibly contain his name—printed in type.

But he thrust the thought away from him and, clutching his five dollars in his pocket, he turned down the street and started along the good scout trail.

CHAPTER VIII

AN ACCIDENT

The latter part of the afternoon found Tom many miles from Bridgeboro, and the trail which had passed through such sordid and pride-racking surroundings back in his home town, now led up through a quiet woodland, where there was no sound but the singing of the birds and an occasional rustle or breaking of a twig as some startled wild creature hurried to shelter.

Through the intertwined foliage overhead Tom could catch little glints of the blue sky, and once, when he climbed a tree to get his bearings, he could see, far in the distance, the lake and the clearing of Temple Camp, and could even distinguish the flagpole.

But no flag flew from it, for the season had not yet begun; Jeb Rushmore was on a visit to his former "pals" in the West, and the camp was closed tight. Down there was where Tom had won the Gold Cross.

He would have liked to see a flag waving, for Bridgeboro, with all its patriotic fervor and bustle, seemed very far away now, and though he was in a country which he loved and which meant much to him, he would have been glad of some tangible reminder that he was, as he had told himself, *with the Colors*.

Tom had left the train at Catskill Landing and reached the hill by a circuitous, unfrequented route, hoping to reach, before dark, the clearer path which he himself had made and blazed from the vicinity of Temple Camp to the little hunting shack upon the hill's summit. This, he felt sure, was the path Roscoe would follow.

It was almost dark when, having picked his way through a very jungle where there was no more sign of path than there is in the sky, he emerged upon the familiar trail at a point about a mile below the shack.

He was breathless from his tussle with the tangled under-brush, his old clothes had some fresh tears, and his hands were cut and bleeding.

For three solid hours he had worked his way up through the tangled forest, and now, as he reached the little trail which was not without its own obstacles, it seemed almost like a paved thoroughfare by contrast.

"Thank goodness!" he breathed. "It's good *he* didn't have to go that way—I—could see *his* finish!"

He was the scout now, the typical scout—determined, resourceful; and his tattered khaki jacket, his slouched hat, his rolled-up sleeves, and the belt axe which he carried in his hand, bespoke the rugged power and strong will of this young fellow who had trembled when Miss Margaret Ellison spoke pleasantly to him.

He sat down on a rock and poured some antiseptic over the scratches on his hands and arms.

Percy K. Fitzhugh

"I can fight the woods, all right," he muttered, "even if they won't let me go off and fight the Germans."

After a few minutes' rest he hurried along the trail, pausing here and there and searching for any trifling sign which might indicate that the path had been recently traveled. Once his hopes of finding Roscoe were dashed by the discovery of a cobweb across the trail, but when he felt of it and found it sticky to the touch he knew that it had just been made.

At last, hard though the ground was, he discovered a new footprint, and presently its meaning was confirmed when he caught a glint of light far ahead of him among the trees.

At the sight of it his heart gave a great bound. He knew now for a certainty that he was right. He had known it all along, but he was doubly assured of it now.

On the impulse he started to run, but his foot slipped upon an exposed root, and as he fell sprawling on the ground his head struck with a violent impact on a big stone.

After a few stunned seconds he dragged himself to a sitting posture; his head throbbed cruelly, and when he put his hand to his forehead he found that it was bleeding. He tried to stand, but when he placed his weight upon his left foot it gave him excruciating pain.

He sat down on the rock, dizzy and faint, holding his throbbing head and lifting his foot to ease, if possible, the agonizing pain.

"I'm all right," he muttered impatiently. "I was a fool to start running; I might have known I was too tired."

That was indeed the plain truth of the matter; he was so

weary and spent that when, in the new assurance of success, he had begun to run, his tired feet had dragged and tripped him.

"That's what—you—get for—hurrying," he breathed heavily; "like Roy always said—more haste—less—Ouch, my ankle!"

He tried again to stand, but the pain was too great, and his head swam so that he fell back on the rock.

"I wish Doc—Carson—was here," he managed to say. Doc was the troop's First-Aid Scout. "It—it was just—because I didn't—lift my feet—like Roy's always telling me—so clumsy!"

He soaked his handkerchief in antiseptic and bound it about his forehead, which was bleeding less profusely. After a few minutes, feeling less dizzy, he stood upon his feet, with a stoical disregard of the pain, determined to continue his journey if he possibly could.

The agony was excruciating, but he set his strong, thick lips tight, and, passing from one tree to another, with the aid of his hands, he managed to get along. More than once he stopped, clinging to a tree trunk, and raised his foot to ease the anguish. His head throbbed with a cruel, steady ache, and the faintness persisted so that often he felt he was about to reel, and only kept his feet by clinging to the trees.

"This—this is just about—the time I'd be going to that—racket—" he said. "Gee, but that foot hurts!"

He would have made a sorry figure on the platform. His old khaki jacket and trousers were almost in shreds. Bloodstains were all over his shirt. A great bloody scratch was visible

Percy K. Fitzhugh

upon his cheek. His hands were cut by brambles. There was a grim look on his dirty, scarred face. I am not so sure that he would have looked any nobler if he had been in the first-line trenches, fighting for Uncle Sam....

CHAPTER IX

ROSCOE JOINS THE COLORS

It was now nearly dark, and Tom worked his way along slowly, hobbling where there were no trees, and grateful for their support when he found them bordering the trail. His foot pained him exquisitely and he still felt weak and dizzy.

At last, after almost superhuman efforts, he brought himself within sight of the dark outline of the shack, which seemed more lonesome and isolated than ever before. He saw that the light was from a fire in the clearing near by, and a smaller light was discernible in the window of the shack itself.

Tom had always stood rather in awe of Roscoe Bent, as one of humble origin and simple ways is apt to feel toward those who live in a different world. And even now, in this altogether strange situation and with all the advantages both of right and courage on his side, he could not repress something of the same feeling, as he approached the little camp.

He dragged himself to within a few feet of the fire and stood clutching a tree and leaning against it as Roscoe Bent, evidently startled, came out and faced him.

Percy K. Fitzhugh

A pathetic and ghastly figure Tom must have looked to the fugitive, who stood staring at him, lantern in hand, as if Tom were some ghostly scarecrow dropped from the clouds.

"It's me—Tom Slade," Tom panted. "You—needn't be scared."

Roscoe looked suspiciously about him and peered down the dark trail behind Tom.

"What are *you* doing here?" he demanded roughly. "Is anybody with you? Who'd you bring—"

"No, there ain't," said Tom, almost reeling. His weakness and the fear of collapsing before he could speak gave him courage, but he forgot the little speech which he had prepared, and poured out a torrent which completely swept away any little advantage of self-possession that Roscoe might have had.

"I didn't bring anybody!" he shouted weakly. "Do you think I'm a spy? Did you ever know a scout that was a *sneak*? Me and you—are all alone here. I knew you was here. I *knew* you'd come here, because you're *crazy*. I seen—saw—"

It was characteristic of Tom that on the infrequent occasions when he became angry, or his feelings got the better of him, he would fall into the old illiterate phraseology of Barrel Alley. He steadied himself against the tree now and tried to speak more calmly.

"D'you think just 'cause you jollied me and made a fool out of me in front of Miss Ellison that I wouldn't be a friend to you? Do you think"—he shouted, losing all control of himself—"that because I didn't know how to talk to you and—and—answer you—like—that I was a-scared of you?

Did you think I couldn't find you easy enough? Maybe I'm—maybe I'm thick—but when I get on a trail—there's—there's nothin' can stop me. I got the strength ter strangle *you*—if I wanted to!" he fairly shrieked.

Then he subsided from sheer exhaustion.

Roscoe Bent had stood watching him as a man might watch a thunderstorm. "You hurt yourself," he said irrelevantly.

"It says in a paper," panted Tom, "that—that a man that's afraid to die ain't—fit to live. D'you think I'd leave—I'd let you—stay away and have people callin' you a coward and a —a slacker—and then somebody—those secret service fellows—come and get you? I wouldn't let them get you," he shouted, clutching the tree to steady himself, "'cause I know the trail, I do—I'm a scout—and *I got here first*—I—"

His hand slipped from the tree, he reeled and fell to the ground too quick for Roscoe to catch him.

"It's—it's all right," he muttered, as Roscoe bent over him. "I ain't hurt.... Roll your coat up tight—you'd know, if you was a scout—and put it under my neck. I—want a drink—of water.... You got to begin right now to-night, Rossie, with the Colors; you got to begin—by—by bein' a Red Cross nurse.... I'm goin' to call you Rossie now—like the fellers in the bank," he ended weakly, "'cause we're friends to each other—kind of."

CHAPTER X

TOM AND ROSCOE COME
TO KNOW EACH OTHER

"I don't know what I said," said Tom; "I was kind of crazy, I guess."

"I guess I'm the one that was crazy," said Roscoe. "Does your head hurt now?"

"Nope. It's a good thick head, that's one sure thing. Once Roy Blakeley dropped his belt-axe on it around camp-fire, and he thought he must have killed me. But it didn't hurt much. Look out the coffee don't boil over."

Roscoe Bent looked at him curiously for a few seconds. It was early the next morning, and Tom, after sleeping fairly well in the one rough bunk in the shack, was sitting up and directing Roscoe, who was preparing breakfast out of the stores which he had brought.

"I guess that's why I didn't get wise when you first asked me about this place—'cause my head's so thick. Roy claimed he got a splinter from my head. He's awful funny, Roy is.... If I'd 'a' known in time," he added impassively, "I could 'a' started earlier and headed you off. I wouldn't 'a' had to stop to chop down trees."

"Why didn't you swim across the brook?" Roscoe asked. "All scouts swim, don't they?"

"Sure, but that's where Temple Camp gets its drinking water —from that brook; and every scout promised he wouldn't ever swim in it. It wasn't hard, chopping down the tree."

Roscoe gazed into Tom's almost expressionless face with a kind of puzzled look.

"It don't make any difference now," said Tom, "which way I came. Anyway, you couldn't of got back yesterday—before the places closed up. Maybe we've got to kind of know each other, sort of, being here like this. You got to camp with a feller if you want to really know him."

Roscoe Bent said nothing.

"As long as you get back to-day and register, it's all right," said Tom. "They'll let you.—It ain't none of my business what you tell 'em. You don't even have to tell me what you're going to tell 'em."

"I can't tell them I just ran away," said Roscoe dubiously.

"It's none of *my* business what you tell 'em," repeated Tom, "so long as you go back *to-day* and register. When you get it over with, it'll be all right," he added. "*I* know how it was— you just got rattled.... The first time I got lost in the woods I felt that way. All you got to do is to go back and say you want to register."

"I said I would, didn't I?" said Roscoe.

"Nobody'll ever know that I had anything to do with it," said Tom.

"Are you sure?" Roscoe asked doubtfully.

"They'd have to kill me before I'd tell," said Tom.

Roscoe looked at him again—at the frowning face and the big, tight-set mouth—and knew that this was true.

"How about *you*?" he asked. "What'll they think?"

"That don't make any difference," said Tom. "I ain't thinkin' of that. If you always do what you know is right, you needn't worry. You won't get misjudged. I've read that somewhere."

Roscoe, who knew more about the ways of the world than poor Tom did, shook his head dubiously. He served the coffee and some crackers and dry breakfast food of which he had brought a number of packages, and they ate of this makeshift repast as they continued their talk.

"You ought to have brought bacon," said Tom. "You must never go camping without bacon—and egg powder. There's about twenty different things you can do with egg powder. If you'd brought flour, we could make some flapjacks."

"I'm a punk camper," admitted Roscoe.

"You can see for yourself," said Tom, with blunt frankness, "that you'd have been up against it here pretty soon. You'd have had to go to Leeds for stuff, and they'd ask you for your registration card, maybe."

"I don't see how I'm going to leave you here," Roscoe said doubtfully.

"I'll be all right," said Tom.

"What will you say to them when you come home?"

"I'll tell 'em I ain't going to answer any questions. I'll say I had to go away for something very important."

"You'll be in bad," Roscoe said thoughtfully.

"I won't be misjudged," said Tom simply; "I got the reputation of being kind o' queer, anyway, and they'll just say I had a freak. You can see for yourself," he added, "that it wouldn't be good for us to go back together—even if my foot was all right."

"It's better, isn't it?" Roscoe asked anxiously.

"Sure it is. It's only strained—that's different from being sprained—and my head's all right now."

"What will you do?" Roscoe asked, looking troubled and unconvinced in spite of Tom's assurances.

"I was going to come up here and camp alone over the Fourth of July, anyway," said Tom. "I always meant to do that. I'll call this a vacation—as you might say. I got to thank *you* for that."

"You've got to thank *me* for a whole lot," said Roscoe ironically; "for a broken head and a lame ankle and missing all the fun last night, and losing your job, maybe."

"I ain't worryin'," said Tom. "I hit the right trail."

"And saved me from being—no, I'm one, anyway, now—"

"No, you ain't; you just got rattled. Now you can see straight, so you have to go back right away. As soon as my foot's better, I'll go down to Temple Camp. That'll be to-morrow— or *sure* day after to-morrow. I'm going to look around the camp and see if everything is all right, and then I'll hike into Leeds and go down by the train. If I was to go limping back, they might think things; and, anyway, it's better for you to get there alone."

"Are you *sure* your foot'll be all right?" Roscoe asked.

"Sure. I'll read that book of yours, and maybe I'll catch some trout for lunch ..."

Roscoe sprang forward impulsively and grasped Tom's hand.

"Now you spilled my coffee," said Tom impassively.

"Tom, I don't know how to take you," Roscoe said feelingly; "you're a puzzle to me. I never realized what sort of a chap you were—when I used to make fun of you and jolly you. Let's feel your old muscle," he added, on the impulse. "I wish *I* had a muscle like that...."

"Tie a double cord around it, and I'll break the cord," said Tom simply.

"I bet you can," said Roscoe proudly, "and—you saved me from ... I don't know what you did it for...."

"I got no objections to telling you," said Tom. "It's because I liked you. There might have been other reasons, but that's the main one. If I only knew how to act and talk—especially to girls—and kind of make them laugh and—"

"Don't talk that way," said Roscoe, sitting on the edge of the bunk and speaking with great earnestness. "You make me feel like a—like a criminal. Me! What am I? You tell Margaret Ellison about how you can break a cord around your arm—and see what she'll say. *That's* the kind of things they like to know about you. You don't know much about them—"

"I never claimed I did," said Tom.

"Here, I'm going to try you—call your bluff," said Roscoe, with a sudden return to that gay impulsiveness which was so natural to him. "Here's the cord from the salmon cans—"

"You should never bring salmon in big cans," said Tom, unmoved. "'Cause it don't keep long after you open it. You should have small cans of everything."

"Yes, kind sir," said Roscoe; "don't try to change the subject. Here, I'm going to try you out—one, two, three."

"You can put it around four times, if you want," said Tom. "Do you know how to tie a brig knot?"

"Me? I don't know anything—except how to be a fool. There!"

Tom slowly bent his bared arm as the resistant cord cut the flesh; for a second it strained, seeming to have withstood the full expanse of his muscle. Then he closed his arm a little more, and the four strands of cord snapped.

"Christopher!" said Roscoe. He towelled Tom's rebellious shock of hair. "Wouldn't it be good if we could go together—to the war, I mean!"

"If it keeps up another year, I'll be eighteen," said Tom.

"Maybe I'll meet you there—you can't tell."

"In that little old French town called—Do you know the most famous town in France?" Roscoe broke off.

Tom shook his head.

"Give it up? *Somewhere*—the little old berg of Somewhere in France. *Wee, wee, messeur—polly voo Fransay?*"

Tom laughed. "There's one thing I wish you'd do," he said. "When I go through Leeds on the way home, I'll stop in the postoffice and you can send me a note to say you registered and everything's all right. Then I'll enjoy the ride in the train better."

"You think I won't register?" said Rocsoe, becoming suddenly sober. "You couldn't stop me now."

"I know it," said Tom; "it ain't that. But I'd just like you to write—will you?"

"I sure will—if I'm not in jail," he added ruefully. "But I don't like to go and leave you here."

"It's the best way, can't you see that?" said Tom. "I won't be in bad with them any more after a couple of days than I am now. And then my foot'll be better. You got to be careful not to mention my name. It's none of my business what you tell 'em about not being there yesterday. I ain't advising anybody to lie. I could get into the army if I wanted to lie; but I promised our scoutmaster.—Just the same, it's none of my business, as long as you register."

"If I broke my word with you," said Roscoe soberly, "I'd be a low-down—"

"You only got about an hour and a half to catch the train," said Tom.

He couldn't think of much else while Roscoe was there.

CHAPTER XI

TOM MEETS A STRANGER

Tom's ankle still pained him more than he had been willing to admit, but the departure of Roscoe for home was a load off his mind, and he felt that now his work was done. In four hours, at most, Roscoe would be back in Bridgeboro, his name upon the rolls, his registration card in his pocket. Tom envied him.

It was exactly like Tom not to worry about how the authorities would receive Roscoe's excuses, or what people would think of his own absence. His mind was a very simple one, and he believed, as he had told Roscoe, that if one did what was right he would not be misjudged.

When the effects of Roscoe's "mistake" had blown over and his own lameness subsided, he would go back to Bridgeboro, and he knew exactly what he was going to say. He was going to say that he had been called away unexpectedly about something very important. That was what business men like Mr. Temple and Mr. Burton and Mr. Ellsworth were always saying—that they were called away; and to be on the safe side, Tom intended to use that very expression. There might be some curiosity and annoyance, but a scout who held the Gold Cross (or at least *owned* it) would not be suspected of doing anything wrong. They would say, "He's an odd number, Tom is," and he would not mind their saying that, for he had heard it before.

During the morning he sat propped up in the bunk reading *Treasure Island*, and in the afternoon he limped out to the brook and caught some minnows, which he fried in cracker crumbs, and had a gala repast all by himself.

While it was still light he decided that he would follow the familiar trail down to Temple Camp and spend the night there. He had the key to the main pavilion, and there he could enjoy the comfort of a couch and a much-needed night's rest. He had left some clothing there, also, which he meant to exchange for his tattered raiment.

He found the camp gloomy enough with all the cabins closed and barred, the rowboats lying inverted on the shore of the lake, and not a soul to welcome him in that beloved retreat which had been the scene of so much fun and adventure. It made him think of Roy and the troop to limp about and see the familiar places, and he sat down on the long rough seat at the bleak-looking mess-board and thought of the past summer, of Jeb Rushmore, of Pee-wee's curly hair and lively countenance, of the scouts trooping from woods and cabin to the grateful evening meal which was served there each night.

Soon, in a week or two perhaps, Jeb would return, and before long that quiet grove would echo to the sound of merry voices. He sat gazing in the twilight at the long, deserted mess-board. How well he remembered the night when all the camp had assembled here in honor of the birthday of the Elk Patrol—*his* patrol!

"If it wasn't for me, this camp would never have been started," he mused proudly; "Mr. Temple saw what scouting could do for a feller, and that's why he started it.... I'm mighty glad I got to be a scout...."

It made him homesick to look about; homesick for the good old times, for Jeb, and the stalking and tracking and swimming, and Roy's jollying of Pee-wee at camp-fire, and the hikes he and Roy used to have together.

"Anyway, I'll see them all to-morrow night at troop meeting," he said to himself, "and in August we'll all be up here again.—I bet they'll laugh and say I was a queer duck to go away—that's what Roy's always saying."

He found some ointment in the provision cabin and rubbed his ankle until his arm was tired. Then he bandaged it and went to bed in one of the comfortable cot-beds in the pavilion.

Early in the morning he was up and glad to find that he could stand upon his injured foot without pain.

The sun was streaming in through the window which he had thrown open, and its cheerful brightness drove away any lingering misgivings which he might have had about Roscoe's or his own reception in Bridgeboro. He donned an old suit of his own which, though faded, was free from tears.

"It's all right now; everything's all right now," he said; "he's registered by now, and to-morrow night I'll show up at troop meeting and they can kid me and say I was afraid to stay and go on the platform—I don't care. I know I hit the right trail. Let 'em call me queer if they want to."

He made breakfast for himself with a pocketful of loose coffee which he had brought down from the mountain and some canned meat which he found in the provision cabin.

Then he hit up through the grove for the road which would take him into the village of Leeds, where he could catch the trolley line for Catskill Landing.

"That was a good job, anyway," he said to himself, as he limped steadily along; "I bet Mr. Bent was glad—Gee, it must be fine to have a father like that!..."

The birds were chattering in the trees along the roadside; hard by a little herd of lazy cows stood in a swamp under a spreading willow like statues of content; now and again an agile chipmunk ran along the stone wall and disappeared into one of its little rocky caverns; in the fields beyond farm hands with great straw hats could be seen at their labors, reminding poor Tom of his own sorry bungling as a war farmer; and the whole tranquil scene was filled with the breath of spring, which entered the soul of Tom Slade as he limped steadily along, and made him feel happy and satisfied.

"Anyway, this is just as good—just as good as being on a committee," he told himself; "I always liked the country best of all, anyway—I always said I did. The scout trail takes you to good places—that's one sure thing."

Presently he passed a bend in the road and discovered some distance ahead of him a figure—evidently that of a youth—trudging along under the weight of a tremendous old-fashioned valise which he carried now in one hand, now in the other, and now again on his shoulder.

In the intervals of changing he laid the valise on the ground, pausing in evident relief. At length, he sat down on a rock, and as Tom approached he screwed up his face in a rueful grin. It was an extraordinary face and such a grin as Tom had never seen before—a grin which made even the scout smile look like drooping despair by comparison. And as for freckles, there were as many of them as there are stars in the peaceful heaven.

"Too much for you?" asked Tom, as he paused by the rock.

The boy made no answer, but shook his head expressively and mopped his forehead.

"I'll help you carry it," said Tom. "We can both get hold of the handle. I got to do a good turn, anyway."

"Sit down and rest," said the stranger. "I got some apples inside, and we'll dig into a couple of 'em. Like apples?"

CHAPTER XII

TOM HEARS OF THE BLOND BEAST

The young fellow was of about Tom's own age, and the most conspicuous thing about him, aside from has smile and his freckles, was the collection of badge-buttons which decorated the lapels of his coat and the front of his hat. They almost rivalled his freckles in number. Some of them were familiar enough to Tom, showing flags and patriotic phrases, but others puzzled him, one or two bearing words which were evidently French. There was an English *Win the War Loan* button, and a Red Cross button which read *I have given two shillings.*

"Here, I'll show you something else," said the stranger, noticing Tom's interest in the buttons. He opened his bag and took out a couple of apples, giving one to Tom. "You see that," he observed, holding up a small crumpled piece of brass. "Know where I got that?" He rolled his R's very noticeably in the manner peculiar to the country people of New York State.

"What is it?" Tom asked.

"It's the cover of an ink-stand. You know what made it like that? A Zeppelin! That was in a raid, that was. It came flying

Percy K. Fitzhugh

plunk out through the front window—and it stuck right into a tree like a dagger. It might have stuck in my head, only it didn't. I'm lucky—that's what our gun crew says." He breathed on the crumpled souvenir and rubbed it on his trousers to polish it. "See, it's got a kind of—initials, like—on it! Everybody has their initials on things in England."

Tom took the little twisted ornamental cover in his hand and gazed at it, fascinated.

"See? M. E. M.," continued the stranger. "That was near Whitehall, it was; a little girl was sitting at a table writing her lessons; she was just in the middle of a word—that's what I heard people in the crowd say—when, kerflunk! down comes, the bomb through the roof and goes right through the floor of the top room and hits right on the table! *Go-o-d-night* for that little girl!"

"Kill her?" Tom asked.

"Blew her all to pieces," said his companion, as he took the poor little trinket and continued to polish it on his knee.

Of all that Tom Slade had read about the war, its grim cruelties, its thousands slain and maimed, its victims struggling frantically in the rough ocean, the poor starving wretches in Belgium, nothing had impressed him so deeply nor seemed to bring the war so close to him as this little crumpled piece of brass—the sad memorial of a little girl who had been blown into eternity while she was studying her lessons. A lump came up in his throat, and he stood watching his companion, and saying nothing.

"That was the blond beast, that was," said the stranger. "I saw him stickin' his old head out of the ocean, too, and we got a pop at him last trip. Here, I'll show you something else."

Out of the bag he drew a photograph. "There; that's our gun crew; that's Tommy Walters—he's the one says I'm a mascot. I'm taking him some apples now. That feller there is Hobart. And that's old Billy Sunday himself, right in the middle," he added, pointing to a long, horizontal object concealed by a canvas cover; "that's him, the bully old boy!"

"A gun, is it?"

"You'd say so if you heard it pop and saw it jump—that's how it got its name."

In the photograph three young men in khaki, one with his sleeves rolled up, were leaning against a steamer's rail.

"Are they Americans?" Tom asked, for he was puzzled about his new friend's nationality.

"You said it."

One of the gun crew was smiling straight at Tom so that he almost smiled back, and the lump came up higher in his throat and his eyes glistened.

"Do you live around here?" he asked. "I'd like to know what your name is and what—and how you—" he broke off.

"You see that house over the hill? I live there. And I'm going back on the job now. What d'ye say we move along?"

They lifted the valise and started along the road.

"This is the last day of my leave," said the youth. "Here,

see?" And he exhibited a steamship card with the name of a steamer upon it and the name of Archibald Archer written in the blank space underneath.

"That's my ship, and I go aboard her to-day, thank goodness! This'll be my third trip across, and the second time I've been home. This bag is half full of apples. Tommy Walters is crazy about 'em. The last trip, when I was home, I took him some russets. He wouldn't let me pop the gun, but he said if the dirty beast came near enough I could let him have the core of an apple plunk in his old periscope. If you were there, we'd sit on the main hatch eatin' apples and watchin' for periscopes. I don't have much to do after I get my berths made up."

"Do you work on the ship?" Tom asked.

"You bet! I'm one of the steward's boys. Gee, if you had to make fifty-seven beds with a life preserver on, you'd know what it is to be tired! Carrying this old suitcase is a cinch compared to that!—Say, if there's a Zep raid in London while I'm there I'll get you a souvenir. But the trouble is they never come when you want 'em to. Do you live in Leeds?"

"I live in Bridgeboro, New Jersey," said Tom, "and my name is Slade. I'd tell you to call me Tom, only I won't know you more than half an hour or so, so what's the use?"

"Half an hour's better than nothing," said Archibald Archer. "Are you on your way home?"

"I just came from the camp," said Tom, side-stepping the real object of his trip. "You know Temple Camp, don't you? I work for Temple Camp."

He was glad that his companion did not pursue his inquiries.

"That's where all the scouts come in the summer, isn't it?" he queried.

"I'm all alone," said Tom. "You're lucky to have a home up in the country to come to. And you're lucky to have a job like that too."

"I told you I was lucky," said Archibald Archer.

They walked on in silence for a little while, carrying the bag between them.

"You've seen something of the war, all right," commented Tom, "and I'll bet you're not eighteen yet. You sure are lucky! I don't blame you for calling Germany the blond beast. I wish *I* could be in it like you."

"Why don't you enlist?"

"I promised I wouldn't—not till I'm eighteen. I got to talk to my scoutmaster about it, 'cause I said I would. I wouldn't lie about how old I am, because he says if a feller lies about one thing he'll lie about another.... I wonder if you'd call it being with the Colors, working like you do?" he added.

"If you saw Old Glory flying from the stern and did your work with a life preserver wrapped around you and spent most of your time piking for subs and practicing emergency drills, just to let old Blondy know he can't stop us from coming across—you'd say you were with the Colors! If you stood where I did and saw that little old periscope topple over like a ninepin and heard Tommy say, 'Go get me another apple, Archie—we'll hit 'em again for good luck!'— you'd say you were with the Colors, all right! You might be in the third-line trenches a whole year an' have nothing to do with yourself but carry buckets and dig in the dirt. *I* know."

Tom was fascinated.

"All you got to do is say the word," his companion went on, reading his thoughts. "The steward'll put you on. They only sign you up for one trip at a time. If you're over sixteen, it's all right. They're taking up the shore passes to-day. Nobody knows when we'll sail, or even where we're going—except the captain. If I say I know you, it'll be all right. You get a hundred and sixty dollars for the trip, and you'll have about two weeks shore leave on the other side. The principal thing they'll tell you is about keepin' your mouth shut. Are you good at that?"

"There's nobody can get anything out of me if I don't want to tell," said Tom doggedly; "and I think you *are* with the Colors. *I* call it being in the war, and it's what I'd like to do, that's one sure thing!"

"I could tell you a lot of things," said Archer, "only I'm not supposed to tell 'em to anybody."

"I got to go home," said Tom; "I'm glad I met you, though. We can go in on the train together, can't we? I have to go to New York to get home. I got to go to scout meeting to-night. I'm going to stop in the postoffice when we get to Leeds; then we'll go down to Catskill Landing together, hey? I'm glad I had company, 'cause I was feeling kind of lonely and queer, like. When you talk it makes me feel as if I'd like to do that, only I see I can't."

Archibald Archer gave a curious look at Tom as they plodded along.

"What you tell me about that little girl makes me want to get into it all the more," Tom said.

CHAPTER XIII

AS OTHERS SAW HIM

In Leeds Tom left his companion sitting on a carriage step in the main street while he went over to the postoffice. As soon as he was out of young Archer's presence the tempter who had been pulling at his elbow left him, and his thoughts flew back to Roscoe and home.

He asked if there was a letter for him, and eagerly took the envelope which the clerk handed out. It was addressed in an unfamiliar, neat bank hand. Anxiously he stepped over to the better light near the window and read:

"DEAR TOM:

"Here I am, and it's twenty-three for mine." (Tom paused in suspense at this ominous phrase.) "My registration card is numbered twenty-three, so I'm the only original skiddoo soldier—take it from your Uncle Dudley.

"When I toddled up to Doc Fuller and told him that I was out of town Wednesday and just couldn't get back, you ought to have seen the look he gave me—over the top of those spectacles of his. I just stood there as if I was on the firing-line facing German clam-shells, and never flinched.

Percy K. Fitzhugh

I wouldn't mind a few Krupp guns now—not after that look.

"But Doc's a pretty good skate—I'll say that for him. He was better than the other members of the Board, anyway.

"Well, I got away with it, all right, only it's good another day didn't slip by, for then my name would have gone in and—g-o-o-d-ni-ight!

"Tommy, you're one brick! When I think of that old towhead of yours and that scowl and that old mug, I know we'll win the war. You'd walk right through that Hindenburg line if you ever got started.

"I've got to hand it to you, Tom—you brought me to my senses, all right, and I won't forget it in a hurry.

"But, Tommy boy, *you're* in Dutch down here—I might as well tell you the truth. And it makes me feel like a criminal. Old Man Temple has got the knife in you. *Greatly disappointed in him*—that's what he told Ellsworth and Pop Burton. Can't you see the old man frowning?

"I went in to put some mail on his desk and the whole three of them were in there pounding away with their little hammers. The old man was as nice as pie to me—patted me on the shoulder and gave me the glad hand. Said I was Uncle Sam's boy now. They didn't even know I wasn't registered Wednesday."

Tom was glad of that. He had succeeded better than he had dreamed. His awe of Roscoe Bent had not entirely vanished, and he was proud to receive so familiar a letter from him. He was so generously pleased that for the moment he did not think of much else. Then he read on:

"Ellsworth said he'd been afraid you would do just what you had done—run off and join the army. He said you promised him you wouldn't, but he guessed you couldn't stand the strain when you saw   the fellows lining up to register.

"A couple of Boy Scouts told Ellsworth they saw you coming out of a pawnshop, and they were chewing that over in the old gent's office. But I guess those kids were dreaming, hey?

"The old gent said he guessed you were afraid to go up on the platform at the rally but didn't like to tell him so. Tom, I never knew you were scheduled for that—why didn't you tell me? You're aces up—you're one bully old trump. I never even knew you till now. You're a brick, you stubborn, tow-headed old forest fighter! You're fourteen-karat and you don't even know it yourself—you're so blamed stupid!"

Tom gulped slightly as he read this and his eyes glistened, but he read on with a kind of stolid indifference:

"I was going to tell them the whole thing, Tom, but I guess I was too mean and too much of a coward. Anyway, I promised you I wouldn't. I hope your ankle is better, and if you can't get home, let me know and I'll come up after you.

"In a hurry,
"Rossie."

"P.S. When Pop Burton told Margaret E. that you had run off to join the army, she said that was splendid. He told

Percy K. Fitzhugh

her you'd have to lie about your age, and she said that was *glorious*. Can you beat that? Old Man Temple went to Chicago to-night, thank goodness, to buy some railroads and things. So long—see you soon."

Tom was glad, he was even proud, that the letter was signed by the familiar nickname, and he was glad of the friendly "So long."

Before he allowed himself to think of anything else he read the letter over again, lingering upon the familiar and humorous phrases which seemed to constitute himself and Roscoe as close friends. The part pertaining to himself he read in a half daze. It seemed to knock the bottom out of his whole theory that he who does right is always safe. Tom's mind, in some ways, was very, very simple, and now that he read the letter in relation to himself it was a knockout blow.

For a few minutes he stood gazing out of the postoffice window, watching two men who were taking down the registration-day decorations from the hotel opposite. A soldier in khaki went by and stopped to chat with them. A farmer came in for his mail, and Tom heard his voice as in a dream.

Then suddenly he shook off his abstraction and walked back to the little grated window.

"I want to get a stamped envelope," he said.

At the writing shelf he tore a sheet out of his scout blank book and wrote:

"DEAR ROSCOE:

"I got your letter and I'm glad you got registered and that

nobody knows. If you had told, it would have spoiled it all.

"I see I did get misjudged, and if they want to think that I tell lies and break promises, let them think so. As long as they think that, anyway, I've decided I will go and help the government in a way I can do without breaking my word to anybody.

"You can see, yourself, I'm not one of the kind that tells lies.

"I've got my mind made up now; I made it up all of a sudden like, as long as that's what they think. So I'm not coming back to Bridgeboro. I'm going away somewhere else. The thing I care most about is that you got registered. And next to that I'm glad because it helped us to get to be friends, because I like you and I always did, even when you made fun of me.

"Your friend,
"TOM."

He put the letter in his pocket, thinking it would be better to mail it from New York. Then he went out and over to where young Archer was sitting.

"I've decided I'll go if you can get me a job," he said "and if you're sure I don't have to tell them I'm eighteen. Maybe you wouldn't call it being in the war exactly, but—"

"Sure you would," Archer interrupted, with great alacrity, "I'll tell you something I didn't tell you before, but you have to keep your mouth shut. We're going to be a transport pretty soon—as soon as the boys begin coming out of the camps. We'll be taking them over by the thousands around next

Percy K. Fitzhugh

November—you see!"

"Do you think they'll take me?" Tom asked.

"They'll grab you—you see!"

To be sure, this assurance of a job was not on very high authority, but it was quite like Tom to place implicit confidence in what this engaging young stranger told him. His faith in people was unbounded.

He sat down on the carriage step beside Archer as if there were nothing extreme or unusual in his momentous decision, and with his usual air of indifference waited for the trolley car which would take them to the station at Catskill Landing.

"What d'you say we hit up a couple more apples?" said Archer.

"Will you have plenty left for Tommy Walters?" said Tom.

"Sure! I got enough to last him right through the danger zone."

"Through the danger zone," Tom mused.

For a few minutes they sat munching their apples in silence.

"There's two reasons," said Tom abruptly. "One is because I just got a letter that shows people think I'm a liar and break promises. The other is on account of what you told me about that little girl. If we take food and things over now and take soldiers over later, I guess that's helping, all right. Anyway, it's better than making badges. In another year I'll be eighteen, and then—"

"Here comes the car," said Archibald Archer.

CHAPTER XIV

TOM GETS A JOB

The momentous step which Tom had resolved to take did not appear to agitate his stolid nature in the least. Nor did he give any sign of feeling disappointment or resentment. His whole simple faith was in young Archer now, and he trusted him implicitly.

He sat in the train, sometimes looking straight ahead and sometimes out at the beautiful Hudson where he had spent so many happy hours in the troop's cabin launch, the *Good Turn*.

After a while he said abruptly, "If a feller does what's right and does a good turn and he gets misjudged, then after that he's got a right to do as he pleases."

His companion did not offer any comment upon this, but looked at Tom rather curiously.

After about ten minutes of silence, Tom observed: "I like mysteries; I'm glad we don't know where we're going. It makes it like a book, kind of. I hope the captain won't tell me."

"You can trust him for that," said Archer; "don't worry!"

*   *   *   *   *

If mystery was what Tom craved, he soon had enough to satisfy him. Indeed, no author of twenty-five-cent thrillers could possibly produce such an atmosphere of mystery as he found when he and young Archer reached the pier in New York.

The steamship company, aided and abetted by Uncle Sam, had enshrouded the whole prosy business of loading and sailing with a delightful covering of romance, and Tom realized, as he approached the sacred precincts, that the departure of a vessel to-day is quite as much fraught with perilous and adventurous possibilities as was the sailing of a Spanish galleon in the good old days of yore.

A high board fence protected the pier from public gaze, and as Tom read the glaring recruiting posters which decorated it he felt that, even if his part in the war fell short of actual military service, he was at last about to do something worth while—something which would involve the risk of his life.

A little door in the big fence stood open and by it sat a man on a stool. Two other men stood near him and all three eyed the boys shrewdly.

"This is the first barbed-wire entanglement," said Archer, as they approached. "You keep your mouth shut, but if you have to answer any questions, tell 'em the truth. These guys are spotters."

"What?" said Tom, a little uneasy.

"Secret Service men—they can tell if your great-grandfather

Percy K. Fitzhugh

was German."

"He wasn't," said Tom.

"Hello, you old spiff-head!" said Archer to the gate-keeper, at the same time laying down his satchel with an air of having done the same thing before. The two Secret Service men opened it and rummaged among its contents, one of them helping himself to an apple.

"You bloomin' grafter!" said Archibald.

"That's all right, Archie," said the other man, likewise helping himself. "It's good to see your smiling phiz back again. Who's your friend?"

"He's goin' in to see the steward," said Archer, "I told him I'd get a feller for the butcher—"

"All the passes are taken up," said the gate-man, as he took Archer's pass. "Everybody's on board, and there's nobody needed."

"Oh, is that so?" said Archer derisively. "Just because everybody's on board it don't prove nobody's needed. I didn't say there was any vacancies."

"He'll only come back out again," said the gate-keeper.

"Oh, will he?" said Archer ironically.

"Let him in," laughed one of the Secret Service men, and as he spoke he pulled Tom's pockets inside out in a very perfunctory way and slapped his clothing here and there. It was evident that young Archer was a favorite. As for Tom, he felt very important.

"Didn't I tell you I was lucky?" Archer said, as he and Tom together lugged the big valise down the pier. "Spiffy's a good sketch—but they're getting more careful all the time. Next sailing, maybe, when we're taking troops over, President Wilson couldn't get by with it.... You heard what he said about all the passes being taken? That means all hands are on board. It don't mean we'll sail to-day—or maybe not to-morrow even. We'll sneak out at night, maybe."

Tom had never been in close proximity to an ocean steamer even in peace times, and the scene which now confronted him was full of interest. Along the side of the pier rose the great black bulk of the mighty ship, beneath the shadow of which people seemed like pygmies and the great piles of freight like houses of toy blocks.

The gangways leading up to the decks were very steep and up and down them hurried men in uniforms. Near a pile of heavy, iron-bound wooden cases several soldiers in khaki strolled back and forth. Tom wondered what was in those cases. Hanging from a mammoth crane was part of the framework of a great aeroplane. Several Red Cross ambulances and a big pile of stretchers stood near by, and he peered into one of the ambulances, fascinated. Tremendous spools, fifteen or more feet in diameter, wound with barbed wire, stood on the pier; there were fifty of them, as it seemed to Tom, and they must have carried miles of barbed wire. There were a lot of heavy, canvas-covered wagons with the letters *U.S.A.* on them, and these were packed with poles and rolls of khaki-colored canvas, which Tom thought might be tents. There were automobiles bearing the same initials, and shovels by the thousand, piled loose, all similarly marked.

There was no doubt that Uncle Sam was getting his sleeves rolled up, ready for business.

Percy K. Fitzhugh

At the foot of one of the gangways Archer had to open his bag again to gratify the curiosity of another man who seemed to know what he was about and who, upon Archer's statement of Tom's errand, slapped Tom here and there in the vicinity of his pockets and said, "All right, Tommy," which greatly increased Tom's veneration for the sagacity of Secret Service men.

"He just meant he knew you wasn't German," said Archer.

He led the way along the deck, down a companionway and through a passage where there were names on the doors, such as *Surgeon, Chief Steward, Chief Engineer, First Mate,* etc. They entered the chief steward's cabin, where a man in uniform sat at a desk with other men standing all about, apparently awaiting orders. When his turn came, Archer said:

"Do you remember, Mr. Cressy, you said you wished you had more youngsters like me in the steward's department? I got you one here. He's a friend of mine. He's just like me—only different."

"Well, thank goodness for *that*," said the chief steward, sitting back and contemplating Archibald with a rather rueful look. "*Did* I say that?"

"Yes, sir, you did. So I brought him; Tom Slade, his name is, and he wants a job. He'd like to be chief engineer, but if he can't be that—"

"Maybe he'd be willing to be butcher's assistant," concluded the steward. "Archer," he added, as he reached for one of several speaking tubes near his desk, "if I thought you'd sink, I'd have you thrown overboard.—How'd you enjoy your visit home?"

A brief talk with some unseen person, to which Tom listened with chill misgivings, and the steward directed his young subordinate to take Tom to the purser's office and, if he got through all right there, to the ship's butcher. He gave Tom a slip of paper to hand to the purser.

The purser's cabin was up on the main deck, and it was the scene of much going and coming, and signing and handing back and forth of papers. A young man sat on a stool before a high desk with a huge open book before him.

"He's the third purser," whispered Archer; "don't you be afraid of *him*."

It was to the third purser that Tom told the history of his life—so far as he knew it; where he was born and when, who his parents were, where they had been born, when and where they had died; whether Tom had ever worked on a ship, whether he had any relatives born in or living in Germany or Austria, whether he had ever been employed by a German, and so on and so on.

All this went down in the big book, in which Tom had a page all to himself, and the last question left a chill upon him as he followed his young companion from the cabin—*Whom to notify in case of accident.*

"Accident," he thought. "That means torpedoing."

But against this was the glad news that for the round trip of presumably a month, he would receive one hundred and sixty dollars, forty dollars payable on arrival in a "foreign port," the balance "on return to an American port."

There would be no call upon this stupendous sum, save what he chose to spend in the mysterious, unknown foreign port, and as Tom reflected on this he felt like the regular story-book hero who goes away under a cloud cf suspicion and comes back loaded with wealth and glory.

CHAPTER XV

THE EXCITED PASSENGER

"They'll turn you down if you have a German-silver watch in your pocket," commented Archer, as they descended another companionway; "or if you had the German measles. Didn't I tell you I'd get you through all right? You stick on the job, and they'll sign you up for transport service—then you'll see some fun."

"I got to thank you," said Tom.

"You notice *I'm* not afraid of any of them?" Archer boasted; "I know how to handle them—I've got them all eating out of my hand—all but the captain. We're like a big family here; that's on account of the danger and there not being many passengers. I understand," he whispered significantly, "that there's some soldiers on board—a few of Pershing's men, I guess."

The butcher's domain seemed to be a long way below decks. It had all the appurtenances of a regular store—chopping block, hangers, etc.—and the butcher himself was a genial soul, who took Tom in hand without any ceremony after the usual banter with the flippant young Archibald, who here took his departure, leaving Tom to his fate.

Percy K. Fitzhugh

"Come up to five-ninety-two on the promenade deck and you can bunk with me—I'll fix it with the deck steward," said Archer; and he was as good as his word, for later Tom joined him in an airy stateroom, opening on the main deck, where they enjoyed a sumptuousness of accommodation quite unusual in the ordinary state of things, but made possible by the very small passenger list.

Indeed, Tom was soon to find that, while discipline was strict and uncompromising, as it always is at sea, there was a kind of spirit of fraternity among the ship's people, high and low, caused no doubt, as Archer had said, by their participation in a common peril and by the barnlike emptiness of the great vessel with freight piled on all the passenger decks and in the most inappropriate places. There was a suggestion of camping about all this makeshift which seemed to have gotten into the spirits of the ship's company and to have drawn them together.

"Now I'll take you down," said the butcher, "and show you the store-rooms and refrigerators—you'll be running up and down these steps a good part of the time."

They were no steps, but an iron ladder leading down from the butcher's apartment to a dark passage, where he turned on an electric light.

"Now, these three doors," he said, "are to the three store-rooms—one, two, three."

Tom followed him into one of the rooms. It was large and delightfully cool and immaculately clean. All around were rows of shelves with screen doors before them, and here were stored canned goods—thousands upon thousands of cans, Tom would have said.

"You won't touch anything in here," his superior told him. "None of this will be used before the return trip—maybe not then. Come in here."

Tom followed him through a passage from this room into another exactly like it. Along the passage were great ice box doors. "Cold storage," his superior observed. "You won't have to go in there much."

"Now here's where you'll get your stuff. It's all alphabetical; if you want tomatoes, go to T; if you want salmon—S. Just like a dictionary. If I send you down for thirty pounds of salmon, that doesn't mean thirty cans—see?"

"Yes, sir," said Tom.

"Make up your thirty pounds out of the biggest cans—a twenty and a ten. There's your opener," he added, pointing to a rather complicated mechanical can-opener fastened to the bulkhead. "Open everything before you bring it up."

"Yes, sir."

He led Tom from one place to another, initiating him in the use of the chopping machine, the slicing machine, etc. "You won't find things very heavy this trip," he said; "but next trip we'll be feeding five thousand, maybe. Now's the time to go to school and learn.—Here's the keys; you must always keep these places locked," he added, as he himself locked one of the doors for Tom. "They were just left open while they were being stocked. Now we'll go up."

That very night, when the great city was asleep and the busy wharves along the waterfront were, for the night's brief interval, dark and lonesome, two tug-boats, like a pair of sturdy little Davids, sidled up to the great steel Goliath and slowly she moved out into midstream and turned her towering prow toward where the Goddess of Liberty held aloft her beckoning light in the vast darkness.

And Tom Slade was off upon his adventures.

Indeed, the first one, though rather tame, had already occurred. He and Archer, having received intimations that the vessel might sail that night, had remained up to enjoy her stealthy nocturnal departure, and the fact that they did not know whether she would leave or not had only added zest and pleasant suspense to their vigil.

They were leaning over the rail watching the maneuvering of the tugs when suddenly a man, carrying a suitcase, came running along the deck.

"We're not sailing, are we?" he asked excitedly, as he passed.

"Looks that way," said Archer.

"Where's the gangway? Down that way?" the man asked, not waiting for an answer.

"He'll have a good big jump to the gangway," said Archer. "I guess he was asleep at the switch, hey? What d'you say if we go down—just for the fun of it?"

"Come ahead," said Tom.

At the opening where the gangway had been several men, including the excited passenger, were gathered. The rail had been drawn across the space, and the ship was already a dozen feet or so from the wharf. Tom and Archer paused in the background, wisely inconspicuous.

"Certainly you can't go ashore—how are you going to get ashore—jump?" asked an officer good-humoredly.

"You can have the gangway put up," insisted the man.

"You're talking nonsense," said the officer. "Can't you see we're out of reach and moving?"

"You'd only have to back her in a yard or two," said the man excitedly.

"What, the ship?" asked the officer, in good-natured surprise; and several other men laughed.

"There's no use my starting without my *a*paratus!" said the passenger, his anger mounting. "It will be here to-morrow morning; it is promised! I was informed the ship would not sail before to-morrow night. This is an outrage—"

"I'm sorry, sir," said the officer.

"There's no use my going without my belongings," the man persisted angrily. "I demand to be put ashore."

"That's impossible, sir."

"It is *not* impossible! This is an unspeakable outrage!"

"The wharf closed this afternoon; notice was posted, sir," said the officer patiently.

"I saw no notice!" thundered the man. "It's of no use for me to go without my belongings, I tell you! I cannot go! This is outrageous! I cannot go! I demand to be put ashore!"

By this time the vessel was in midstream, his "demands"

becoming more impossible every moment and his tirade growing rather wearisome. At least that was what most of the by-standers seemed to think, for they sauntered away, laughing, and the two boys, seeing that nothing sensational was likely to happen, returned to the forward part of the ship.

"Do you think he was a German?" said Tom.

"No, sure he wasn't. Didn't you hear what good English he talked?"

"Yes, but he said *a*paratus," said Tom, "instead of saying it the regular way. And he was sorry he said it, too, because the next time he said *belongings*."

"You make me laugh," said Archer.

"There's another thing that makes me think he's a German," said Tom, indifferent to Archer's scepticism.

"What's that?"

"He wanted the ship brought back just on his account."

CHAPTER XVI

TOM MAKES A DISCOVERY

Tom slept fitfully in his upper berth, thinking much of home and the troop and the people back in Bridgeboro. He realized now, as he had not before, the seriousness of the step he had taken. It came home to him in the quiet of the long night and tinged his thoughts with homesickness.

Once, twice, in his restlessness, he clambered down and looked out through the brass-bound port-hole across the deserted deck and out upon the waste of ocean. Not a single reminder was there of the old familiar life, not a friendly light in the vast, watery darkness.

He began to regard what he had done as a kind of wilful escapade, and though not exactly sorry for the action, he felt strange and lonesome, and his thoughts turned wistfully to the troop meeting which he knew was now over. He thought of Pee-wee, with his trusty belt-axe, going scout-pace up Main Street on his journey homeward; of Roy leaving Mr. Ellsworth where the street up Blakeley's Hill began; of the office and Margaret Ellison, and of his accustomed tasks.

No, he was not exactly sorry, but he—he wished that the vessel had not started quite so soon, and so suddenly. He had

Percy K. Fitzhugh

never dreamed that the momentous and perilous step of crossing the ocean was begun with so little ceremony.

This train of thought suggested the passenger who had wished to go ashore, and as Tom lay in his berth, wakeful but pleasantly lulled by the slow, steady vibration of the great ship, he wondered who the man was and why he couldn't sail without his belated luggage. He recalled how the man had said *a*paratus once and how, after that, he had said *belongings*. Then he recalled young Archer's laugh at his suspicion, and he decided that it was only his own imagination that had given rise to it. He thought rather wistfully how Roy had often called him Sherlock Nobody Holmes.

To be sure, the man's apparent willingness to have the world turned upside down for his personal convenience had quite a German flavor to it, but it was not, after all, a very suspicious circumstance, and the cheerful light of morning found Tom's surmise quite melted away. It needed only the memory of Roy's taunting smile to turn his thoughts to sober realities.

"When you get through, come aft and we'll jolly the gun crew," said Archer, as Tom left the little room.

He made his way along the deck, bent on his new duties, bucking the brisk morning breeze, and holding on to the peaked service cap which he had been given, to keep it from blowing off. The steel-colored water rolled in a gentle swell, reflecting the bright sunlight, and little flaky clouds scurried across the sky, as if hurrying to their day's tasks also. Far off toward the horizon a tiny fleck of white was discernible, but no other sign of life or of man's work was visible in the illimitable waste.

To Tom it did not seem an angry ocean, but, like the woods

which he knew and loved so well, a place of peace and quietude, a refuge from the swarming, noisy land. And across the vast waste plowed the great ship, going straight upon her business, and never faltering.

The door of the wireless room was thrown open as he passed, and the young operator was sitting back, with the receivers on his ears and his feet on the instrument shelf, eating a sandwich.

"H'lo, kiddo," said he.

In this strange environment Tom was glad to hear the operator say, "H'lo, kiddo," just as he might have said it on the street. He paused at the door for a moment and looked about the cozy, ship-shape little room with its big coil and its splendid, powerful instrument.

"Do you live in here?" he asked.

"Nope," said the operator; "but I'm doing both shifts, and I s'pose I'll have to sleep right here with the claps on this trip."

"Isn't there another operator?" Tom asked.

"Yup—but he didn't show up."

Tom hesitated, not sure whether he ought to venture further in familiar discourse with this fortunate and important young man, whom he envied.

"The man at the gate said everybody was on board," he finally observed; "he said all the passes were taken up."

The operator shrugged his shoulders indifferently. "I don't know anything about that," said he.

"*I* got a wireless set of my own," Tom ventured. "It's just a small one—for boy scouts. It hasn't got much sending power."

"*He* used to be a boy scout," said the operator pleasantly. "That's where he first picked it up."

"The other operator?"

"Yup."

"I learned some myself," said Tom.

The operator did not seem inclined to talk more, and Tom went along the deck where a few early risers were sauntering back and forth enjoying the fresh morning breeze. He noticed that life preservers were laid across the rail loosely tied and that others stood in little piles at intervals along the deck, loosely tied also.

He ate his breakfast in messroom No. 2 with the deck stewards and their boys and greatly enjoyed it, though his thoughts more than once turned enviously to the wireless operator. After breakfast he went down into his own domains, where, according to instructions, he took from a certain meat-hook a memorandum of what he was to bring up from below.

Descending the dark companionway, he turned on the electric light, and stood puzzled for a moment, paper in hand.

"That's just exactly like me," he said. "I got to admit it."

The fact was that despite his tour of initiation under the butcher's guidance he was puzzled to know which of the two doors opened into the room from which supplies were for the present to be drawn. At a hazard he opened one of them, and on entering did not immediately perceive the room to be the wrong one.

Sliding open one of the screen doors, he stooped and lifted out a couple of cans from a lower shelf. As he did so he heard the usual, unmuffled ticking which was pretty sure to accompany the stooping posture with Tom and which always notified him that his big trusty nickel watch was dangling on its nickel chain.

But it was not dangling this time, and Tom paused in surprise, for the ticking continued quite audibly and apparently very close to him. He took out his watch and held it to his ear, and was surprised to find that its sound was quite distinct from another and slower ticking somewhere near by.

He looked about for a clock, but could see none.

"Huh, that's funny," he said, still listening.

Then, of a sudden, he lifted several more cans from the shelf and knelt down, holding his ear close to the space. From somewhere behind the cans came the steady tick, tick, tick, tick, tick....

For a moment he knelt there in surprise. Then hurriedly he lifted out can after can until there lay revealed upon the shelf a long, dark object. The ticking was louder now.

He touched the object gingerly, and found that it was held fast in place by a wire which ran from a screw in the shelf to another screw in the bulkhead above it, and was thus effectually prevented from moving with the rolling of the ship. Some excelsior lay upon the shelf, which had evidently been stuffed between the ticking object and the back row

Percy K. Fitzhugh

of cans.

Something—Tom did not know just what, but some sudden presentiment—prompted him to step quickly through the passage in order to make sure that he had entered the right room. Then he discovered his mistake.

The room he had entered was the store-room from which no supplies were to be taken on the present trip.

He turned back and knelt again, the cans he had removed standing all about him. One of them, which in his haste he had laid upon its side, began to roll with the jarring of the vessel, and Tom shuddered with a kind of panic fright at the sudden noise it made, and with trembling hands he set the innocent can upright.

Tick, tick, tick, tick....

What did it mean? What should he do?

His next impulse was to run upstairs and report what he had discovered. He did not dare to touch the thing again.

Then he realized that something—something terrible—might happen while he was gone. Something might happen in five minutes—the next minute—the next second!

Still kneeling, for strangely he could not bring himself to move, he watched the thing in a sort of fascination.

Tick, tick, tick, tick, tick—it went, on its steady, grim journey toward—

Toward what?

Still Tom did not budge.

Tick, tick, tick, tick, tick, tick—it went; heedless, cheerful, like a clock on a mantelpiece.

And still Tom Slade remained just where he was, stark-still and trembling.

CHAPTER XVII

ONE OF THE BLOND BEAST'S WEAPONS

Then, of a sudden, Tom Slade, ship's boy, disappeared, and there in his place was Tom Slade, scout; calm, undismayed —the same Tom Slade who had looked about him, calm and resourceful, when he was lost in the great woods, and who had kept his nerve when menaced by a savage beast.

He cautiously removed the encircling wire, lifted the object out with both hands, finding it surprisingly heavy, and laid it carefully upon the stationary table where cans were usually assorted and opened.

Tick, tick, tick, tick, tick—it went cheerfully along on its tragic errand.

It appeared to consist of a piece of ordinary stovepipe about twelve inches long. The face and works of an alarm clock, being of a slightly smaller circumference, had been placed within one end of the pipe, the face out, and the intervening space around this was packed with cotton waste. The other end of the pipe was closed with a kind of gummy cement.

Tom observed that the little alarm dial in the clock's face was set for nine o'clock, which of course afforded him infinite relief, for it was not yet seven.

With the greatest of care and hands trembling a little, he pulled out some of the cotton waste around the clock face, holding the dial steady with one hand, and found that nothing save this packing was holding the clock in place. He joggled it very gently this way and that to make sure that it was not connected with anything behind. Then he lifted it out and stood it upright on a shelf with cans on either side of it to keep it in place.

Tick, tick, tick, tick, tick, tick—it went just as before, as if not in the least disappointed that its tragic purpose had been thwarted; tick, tick, tick, tick—like the old alarm clock that used to stand on the shelf above the sink in Barrel Alley.

There was no Gold Cross for this little act of Tom's, and no "loud plaudits," as Pee-Wee would have said, but Tom Slade had saved a couple of hundred lives, just the same.

It occurred to him now that pretty soon he would be expected upstairs. The hands of the clock pointed to a quarter of six and Tom's own watch, which was as honest, plain and reliable as he was himself, said twelve minutes of seven.

"That's funny," said he.

He peered into the open space which the removal of the clock had left in the pipe's end. It ran for about four or five inches, where the pipe appeared to be sealed with the same gummy substance as at the other end.

On the inside of the pipe was a rough-looking, yellowish area about two inches square, and from this two black, heavy cords ran to the cement wall.

Tom understood at once the mechanism of this horrible thing. The bell of the alarm clock had been removed, and the clock so placed that at the fatal tick the striker would have vibrated against this rough area, which was probably inflammable like a match-end and which, on being ignited, would have ignited the fuse.

Tom's imagination traced the hurrying little flames, racing along those two cords to see which would get there first, and he shuddered, thinking of the end of that sprightly little race to the awful goal....

His lip curled a little as he looked at the now harmless piece of junk and as his eyes wandered to the impenitent clock which, without any vestige of remorse or contrition, was ticking merrily up there on the shelf, out of harm's way between the sentinels of cans.

"Huh, I don't call that fighting!" he said.

Tom's knowledge of war was confined to what he had learned at school. He knew about the Battle of Bunker Hill and that ripping old fight, the Battle of Lexington. These two encounters represented what he understood war to be.

When Mr. Ellsworth had taken him in hand, he had told him a few things known to scouts: that it was cowardly to throw stones; that it was contemptible to strike a person in the back or below the waist; that fighting was bad enough, but that if fights must be fought they should be fought in the open. That a boy should never, *never* strike a girl....

And what kind of fighting was this? thought Tom. Was it not exactly like the boy who sneaks behind a fence and throws stones?

"That ain't fighting," he repeated.

Methodically he went upstairs. His immediate superior was "Butch," but his ultimate superior was Mr. Cressy, the steward; and to him he now went.

"I got somethin' to tell you, Mr. Cressy," he said hurriedly. "I made a mistake and went into the wrong room, and there's a bomb there. It was set for nine o'clock. I fixed it so's it can't go off."

"What?" ejaculated the steward.

"I fixed it so it can't go off," Tom repeated dully. "If I'd waited till I told you, it might 'a' gone off by mistake."

His manner was so entirely free from excitement that for a moment the steward could only stare at him.

"There ain't any danger now," said Tom.

The steward whistled to himself thoughtfully.

"Go down there and wait till I come, and don't say anything about this to anybody," said he.

Tom went down, feeling quite important; he was being drawn head and shoulders into the war now. Once the thought occurred to him that perhaps he would be suspected of something. For he thought he knew now how easily people did "get misjudged." But that seemed absurd, and he dismissed the thought of it—just as he had dismissed the thought of Roscoe Bent's really doing anything wrong or cowardly.

But still a vague feeling of uneasiness held him....

Percy K. Fitzhugh

CHAPTER XVIII

SHERLOCK NOBODY HOLMES

In a few minutes the steward came down with the captain and the first officer and a man in civilian's clothes, who carried a cigar in the corner of his mouth and who Tom thought must be of the Secret Service. Tom stood greatly in awe of the captain, who seemed the very type of exalted dignity. But a cat may look at a king, and he stared at that autocrat, resolved to answer manfully whatever questions were asked him.

"Confirms your suspicions, eh?" said the captain to the man in plain clothes, after a gingerly inspection of the ominous piece of stove pipe.

"Hmmm," said the other man; "yes; no doubt of it. Wish I'd taken him up last trip when he sent that message. We'll have a job finding him now."

"I don't see how he could have got ashore since nine o'clock last night," said the first officer.

"Well, he did, anyway," said the Secret Service man; "they're getting by every day, and they will until we have martial law along the waterfront. You see, this is where he had to come through to his locker," he added, looking about.

The captain gave a brief order to the first officer to have the vessel searched at once for more bombs. The officer hurried away and presently came back again. The Secret Service man was intently examining the floor, the jamb around the door, and the casing of the port-hole. The captain, too, scrutinized the place, as if he hoped it might yield some valuable information; and Tom, feeling very awkward, stood silently watching them.

"Here you are," said the Secret Service man, indicating a brown stain on the door jamb.

The other three men stepped over to the spot, but Tom, who did not dare to join them, stood just where he was, looking uncouth and out of place in the ill-fitting white duck jacket and blue peaked service cap which had been given him.

"There you are, Captain," said the Secret Service man; "see that finger-mark? The skin lines aren't as clear, see? That's from constant pressure. That's the finger he uses to press his wireless key."

"Hmm," said the captain.

"I've had my eye on that young operator for the last two trips," said the plain-clothes man; "he's undoubtedly the fellow who sent that code message that tipped Ekler off and posted him about the *Republic's* sailing, I never liked his name—Hinnerman. We might have known he wouldn't show up for this trip."

"He was a hold-over on board," said the first officer, "and didn't come in for the government quiz. They should have all been thrown out.—Think the other operator's all right?"

he added.

"Oh, yes; he's got two brothers in military service," said the captain conclusively.

"See, here's another finger-mark—thumb. And here's a couple more," said the plain-clothes man, indicating several less distinguishable marks around the port-hole.

No one paid any attention to Tom. He watched the four men as they examined the little signs which they thought verified their conclusion that the missing wireless operator had placed the bomb.

"You see, he knew this room wouldn't be used, probably not entered this trip," said the Secret Service man.

"It was a lucky mistake this boy made," said the first officer, glancing not unkindly at Tom.

"Mmmm," said the captain.

Tom did not know whether to take this for praise or not. He stood, silent but very thoughtful. None of his four superiors took the trouble to acknowledge his act, nor even to address him, and he had to piece together as best he could, from their conversation, the reasons for their long-standing suspicions of the missing operator's disloyalty. Never in all his life had Tom felt his own insignificance as he did now.

The Secret Service man was very self-confident and very convincing. His conclusions, in view of past suspicions, seemed natural enough, and Tom could not help envying and admiring him from his obscure corner.

"I'll send a wireless right away," said the captain, as the four moved toward the door.

For a few seconds Tom struggled to master his timidity. He felt just as he had felt when he talked to Margaret Ellison and when he had faced Roscoe Bent's father. These uniformed officials were as beings from another world to poor Tom, and the Secret Service man seemed a marvel of sagacity and subtle power.

As they reached the door, he spoke, his voice shaking a little, but in the slow, almost expressionless way which was characteristic of him.

"If you'd wait a minute, I got something to say," he said.

"Yes, sir," said the first officer not unpleasantly. The captain paused impatiently. The Secret Service man smiled a little. Indeed, there was plenty to smile at (for the captain, too, if that dignitary would have so condescended) for Tom's sleeves, which were ridiculously long, were clutched in his two hands as if to keep them from running away and the peak of his cap was almost over his ear instead of being where it belonged.

"I heard this morning," said Tom, "that the other operator— the one that isn't here—that he used to be a scout. I'm a scout, and so I know what kind of fellers scouts are. They ain't traitors or anything like that. Something happened to me lately, so I know how easy it is to get misjudged. If he was a scout, then he wasn't a German, even if he might have had a German name, 'cause Germans stay by themselves and don't join in, kind of...."

The captain made a move as if to go.

"But that ain't what I wanted to say," said Tom.

The captain paused.

There was something about Tom's blunt, plain-speech and slow manner which amused the first officer, and he listened with rather more patience, than the others.

"There was a man tried to get off the ship last night," said Tom. "He—"

"Oh, yes, that was Doctor Curry from Ohio," laughed the first officer indulgently. "I hunted him up on the purser's list —*he's* all right. He flew off the handle because his baggage didn't come. He's all right, boy."

"The man that started the English scouts," said Tom, undaunted, "says if you want to find out if a person is foreign, you got to get him mad. Even if he talks good English, when he gets excited he'll say some words funny like."

The captain turned upon his heel.

"But that ain't what I was going to say, either," said Tom dully. "Anybody that knows anything about wireless work knows that operators have to have exactly the right time. That's the first thing they learn—that their watches have got to be exactly right—even to the second. I know, 'cause I studied wireless and I read the correspondence catalogues."

"Well?" encouraged the Secret Service man.

But it was pretty hard to hurry Tom.

"The person that put that bomb there," said he, "probably started it going and set it after he got it fixed on the shelf; and he'd most likely set it by his own watch. You can see that clock is over an hour slow. I was wonderin' how anybody's watch would be an hour slow, but if that Doctor Curry came from Ohio maybe he forgot to set his watch ahead in Cleveland. I know you have to do that when you come east, 'cause I heard a man say so."

A dead silence prevailed, save for the subdued whistling of the Secret Service man, as he scratched his head and eyed Tom sharply.

"How old are you, anyway?" said he.

"Seventeen," said Tom. "I helped a feller and got mis-judged," he added irrelevantly. "A scout is a brother to every other scout—all over the world. 'Specially now, when England and France are such close partners of ours, like. So I'm a brother to that wireless operator, if he used to be a scout.—Maybe I got no right to ask you to do anything, but maybe you'd find out if that man's watch is an hour slow. Maybe you'd be willing to do that before you send a wireless."

The captain looked full at Tom, with a quizzical, shrewd look. He saw now, what he had not taken the trouble to notice before: a boy with a big mouth, a shock of rebellious hair, a ridiculously ill-fitting jacket, and a peaked cat set askew. Instinctively Tom pulled off his cap.

"What's your name?" said the captain.

"Tom Slade," he answered, nervously arranging his long arms in the troublesome, starched sleeves. "In the troop I—used to belong to," he ventured to add, "they called me Sherlock Nobody Holmes, the fellers did, because I was interested in deduction and things like that."

For a moment the captain looked at him sternly. Then the

Percy K. Fitzhugh

Secret Service man, still whistling with a strangely significant whistle, stepped over to Tom.

"Put your cap on," said he, "frontways, like that; now come along with me, and we'll see if Doctor Curry from Ohio can accommodate us with the time."

He put his arm over Tom's shoulder just as Mr. Ellsworth used to do, and together they left the store-room. It seemed to Tom a very long while since any one had put an arm over his shoulder like that....

CHAPTER XIX

THE TIME OF DAY

When that flippant youth, Archibald Archer, making his morning rounds from stateroom to stateroom, beheld Tom Slade hurrying along the promenade deck under the attentive convoy of one of Uncle Sam's sleuths, he was seized with a sudden fear that his protege was being arrested as a spy.

But Tom was never farther from arrest in all his life. He hurried along beside his companion, feeling somewhat apprehensive, but nevertheless quite important.

The federal detective was small and agile, with a familiar, humorous way about him which helped to set Tom at ease. He had a fashion of using his cigar as a sort of confidential companion, working it over into one corner of his mouth, then into the other, and poking it up almost perpendicularly as he talked. Tom liked him at once, but he did not know whether to take literally all that he said or not.

"Long as you told me your name, I guess I might as well tell you mine, hey? Conne is my name—Carleton Conne. Sounds like a detective in a story, don't it? My great-great-grandfather's mother-in-law on my sister's side was German. I'm trying to live it down."

"What?" said Tom.

Mr. Conne screwed his cigar over to the corner of his mouth and looked at Tom with a funny look.

"You see, we want to meet the doctor before he has a chance to change his watch," said Mr. Conne more soberly. "If he set that thing a little after nine last night (and he couldn't have set it before), he was probably too busy thinking of getting off the ship to think of much else. And he ought to be just coming out of his stateroom by now. We must see him before he sees a clock. You get me?"

"Yes, sir," said Tom, a little anxious; "but I might be wrong, after all."

"Maybe," said Mr. Conne. "There are three things we'll have to judge by: There's his trying to get off the ship last night, and there's the question of how his watch stands, and there's the question of how he acts when we talk with him—see?"

"Yes, sir."

"Since you're a detective, remember this," Mr. Conne added good-humoredly: "it's part of the A B C of the business. Three middle-sized clues are better than one big one—if they hang together. Six little ones aren't as good as three middle-sized ones, because sometimes they seem to hang together when they don't really—see?"

"Yes, sir."

"Where'd you ever get your eyes and ears, anyway?" said Mr. Conne abruptly.

"You learn to be observant when—you're a scout," said Tom.

Mr. Conne moved briskly along the deck, and Tom kept beside him with his rather clumsy gait. Here and there little groups of passengers stood chatting as they waited for breakfast. Among them were a few men in khaki whom Tom understood to be army surgeons and engineers—the fore-runners of the legions who would "come across" later.

"Which would you rather be," queried Mr. Conne, "a detective or a wireless operator?"

"I'd rather be a regular soldier," said Tom; "I made up my mind to it. I'm only waiting till I'm eighteen."

Mr. Conne gave him a shrewd sideways glance, his cigar pointing upward like a piece of field artillery.

"But I hope I can work on this ship when she's a regular transport, and keep working on her till I'm eighteen."

"You haven't answered my question yet."

"I don't know which I'd rather be," said Tom.

"Hmmm," said Mr. Conne.

At the after-companionway he picked up a deck steward and asked him to point out Dr. Curry, if he was about.

"What do you suppose became of the other operator?" Tom asked, a little anxiously.

"I don't know," said Mr. Conne. "We'll have to find some one who does know," he added significantly, and Tom wondered what he meant.

"Do you think he's guilty of anything?" he asked.

"Don't know. You've knocked my theories all endways, young fellow," Mr. Conne said pleasantly; and then he added, smiling, "You say he was a scout; I'm getting to have a pretty good opinion of scouts."

"But those finger-prints—"

"Were his," concluded Mr. Conne.

Tom was greatly puzzled, but he said nothing. Soon Dr. Curry was pointed out to them. He was pacing up and down the deck, and paused at the rail as they neared so that they were able to get a good look at him. He was tall and thin, with a black mustache and a very aristocratic hooked nose. Perhaps there was the merest suggestion of the foreigner about him, but nothing in particular to suggest the German unless it were a touch of that scornfully superior air which is so familiar in pictures of the Kaiser.

"So that's the Doctor, is it?" Mr. Conne commented, eyeing him with his cigar cocked up sideways. "Looks kind of savage, huh?"

But the doctor's savage mien did not phase Mr. Conne in the least, for he sauntered up to him with a friendly and familiar air, though Tom was trembling all over.

"Excuse me, would you oblige me with the time?" Mr. Conne said pleasantly.

The stranger wheeled about suddenly with a very pronounced military air and looked at his questioner.

"The time? Yes, sir," he said, with brisk formality and taking out his watch. "It is just half-past six."

Mr. Conne drew out his own watch and looked at it for a moment as if perplexed. "Then one of us is about an hour out of the way," he said sociably, while Tom stood by in anxious suspense. "According to the alarm clock down in the store-room, I guess *you're* right," he added.

"What?" said the passenger, disconcerted.

"According to the time-bomb down below," repeated Mr. Conne, still sociably but with a keen, searching look. "What's the matter? You suffering from nerves, Doctor?"

The sudden thrust, enveloped in Mr. Conne's easy manner, had indeed taken the doctor almost off his feet.

"I do not understand you, sir," he said, with forbidding dignity and trying to regain his poise.

"Well, then, I'll explain," said Mr. Conne; "you forgot to set your watch when you left Cleveland, Doc, so there won't be any explosion down below at nine o'clock, and there won't be any at all—so don't worry."

He worked his cigar over into the corner of his mouth and looked up at his victim in a tantalizing manner, waiting. And he was not disappointed, for in the angry tirade which the passenger uttered it became very apparent that he was a foreigner. Mr. Conne seemed quietly amused.

"Doc," said he sociably, almost confidentially, "I believe if it hadn't been for this youngster here, you'd have gotten away with it. It's too bad about your watch being slow—German reservists and ex-army officers ought to remember when they're traveling that this is a wide country and that East is East and West is West, as old brother Kipling says. When you're coming across Uncle Sam's backyard to blow up ships, it's customary to put your watch an hour ahead in Cleveland, Doc. Didn't they tell you that? Where's all your German efficiency? Here's a wideawake young American youngster got you beaten to a stand-still—"

"This is abominable!" roared the man.

"Say that again, Doc," laughed Mr. Conne. "I like the way you say it when you're mad. So that's why you didn't get off the ship in time last night, eh?" he added, with a touch of severity. "Watch slow! Bah! You're a bungler, Doc! First you let your watch get you into a tight place, then you let it give you away.

"I don't know who you are, except you came from west of Cleveland; but here's an American boy, never studied the German spy system, and, by jingoes, he's tripped you up—and saved a dozen ships and a half a dozen munition factories, for all I know. German efficiency—bah! The Boy Scouts have got you nailed to the mast! This is the kind of boys we're going to send over, Doc. Think you can lick 'em?"

Tom was blushing scarlet and breathing nervously as the fierce, contemptuous gaze of the tall man was bent for a brief second upon him. But Mr. Conne winked pleasantly at him, and it quite nullified that scornful look.

Then, suddenly, the detective became serious, interrupting the stranger, who had begun to speak again, and brushing his words aside.

"You'll have to show me your passport, sir," he said, "and any other papers you have. I'll go to your stateroom with you. Then I'm going to lock you up. I'll expect you to tell me, too, what became of the young fellow who happened to discover you down below last night. You and he had a little scuffle down there, I take it.—Better run along about your duties now, Tom, and I'll see you later."

Percy K. Fitzhugh

CHAPTER XX

A NEW JOB

For a few moments Tom stood gaping at the receding figures, with Mr. Conne's remark ringing in his ears: *I shall expect you to tell me what became of the young fellow who happened to discover you down below last night.*

Was that the possible explanation of the missing wireless boy? The thought of this complication shocked him. What could it mean? The detective had evidently fitted the whole thing together.

Finger-prints were finger-prints, thought Tom, and a finger-print with illegible markings in the center meant a telegraph operator, so far as this particular incident was concerned. He so greatly admired Mr. Conne that as usual he forgot to admire himself....

The man must have been discovered, either in the act of placing the bomb, or perhaps of trying to remove it when he found that he must sail with the ship, and there had been a scuffle and—

And what? Where was the wireless boy?

Alas, though the spy was apprehended, it was to be many long months before the mystery of the missing wireless boy should be cleared up. And who, of all the people in the world, do you suppose cleared it up? Who but Pee-wee Harris (don't laugh) and his trusty belt-axe. But that is part of another story.

The arrest of "Dr. Curry" as a German spy and plotter was a nine hours' wonder on the ship, and the part which Tom Slade had played in the affair did not pass without comment. Neither the ship's officers nor Mr. Conne took him into their confidence as to the character of the papers found on the "doctor," but he understood that that scornful personage was safely lodged somewhere "below," and Mr. Conne did go so far as to tell him that "our friend" had set his watch right. Tom did not dare to ask questions, even of his friend the detective, who chatted pleasantly with him whenever they met.

He was the last boy in the world to expect more consideration than was due him or to make much of his own exploits, and if his superiors did not take him into partnership and make him their confidant and adviser, as undoubtedly they would have done in a story, they at least treated him with rather more consideration than is usually given to ships' boys, and the awkward young fellow in the ill-fitting duck jacket and peaked hat askew was pointed out among the army men and passengers, as he occasionally passed along the decks, as one who had a head on his shoulders and a pair of eyes in his head.

No one questioned that he had saved the vessel by making known the clew which had sent Dr. Curry to the ship's lock-up, and Tom, satisfied to have done something worth while for Uncle Sam, attended to his menial duties, and did not think of very much else.

But if Uncle Sam's Secret Service man had thought it best not to be too confidential with him, kind Fate decreed that it should be Tom Slade and none other who should clinch the case against this foreign wretch whose plans he had thwarted.

It happened the very next day, beginning with a circumstance which made Tom feel indeed like a hero in a cheap thriller.

"The captain wants to see you," said a young officer from the bridge, as Tom sat with his flippant but now humble admirer, Archibald Archer, upon one of the after-hatches.

"Me?" stammered Tom.

"He's going to make you first mate," said Archer, "and give you ten thousand dollars—go ahead."

"What?" said Tom.

"That's the way they do in the *Dick Dauntless Series*; go ahead—beat it!"

Tom followed the officer forward and up those awful steps which led to the holy of holies where the master of the ship held his autocratic sway.

The captain sat in a sumptuously furnished cabin, and Tom stood before him, holding his cap in one hand, clutching his long, starched sleeve with the other, and greatly awed at the surroundings.

"You said something about understanding wireless," said the captain. "Do you think you could be of assistance to the operator?"

"I ain't—I'm not an operator," stammered Tom, "but I know the American code and the International code and some of the International abbreviations. I can send and receive with my own instrument, but it's a kind of—not exactly a toy, but—"

"Hmm. What I mean is, could you work under the operator's direction, so that he could get a little sleep now and then? He'd sleep right in the wireless room."

Tom hesitated.

"I don't—I don't know if I should say, Aye, aye, sir—I hear some of 'em doin' that," said Tom awkwardly.

"You mean, yes, you can?" said the captain, with the faintest suggestion of a smile.

"Yes, I—as long as he's right there with me—yes, sir, I think I could."

"Well, then, you go down there now, and I'll notify the steward."

Tom half turned, then hesitated, clutching his sleeve tighter. "I—I got to thank you," said he.

The captain nodded. "All right; keep your mouth shut, do your best, don't make mistakes, and remember we're at war. And maybe we'll have to thank you," he added.

"It's—it's helping in the war, isn't it?" Tom asked.

The captain nodded. For a moment Tom had a wild notion of asking whether he might continue in the wireless room when the ship was taken over for regular transport service, but he did not dare.

Those who saw him as he went back along the deck saw only the stolid-looking, awkward young fellow in the stiff white jacket three sizes too large for him who had come to be a familiar figure about the ship. And they did not know that the heart of Tom Slade was beating again with hope and joy just as it had beat when he had listened to Mr. Temple and when he stood looking down from the office window into Barrel Alley. And if his hopes and triumphs should be dashed again, they would not know that either ...

On the deck he met Mr. Conne.

"Well, I see the captain beat me to it," said he. "I was thinking of working you into secret service work, but never mind, there's time enough."

"Maybe I won't satisfy them; sometimes I make mistakes," said Tom. "I made a mistake when I went into the wrong store-room, if it comes to that. They always called me Bull-head, the fellers in the troop did."

Mr. Conne cocked his head sideways, screwed his cigar over to the extreme corner of his mouth, and looked at Tom with a humorous scrutiny.

"Did they?" said he. "All right, Tommy, Uncle Sam and I mean to keep our eyes on you, just the same."

So at last the cup of joy was full again—and that same night it overflowed. For as Tom Slade sat at the wireless table, while his new companion slept in his berth near by, there jumped before his eyes a blue, dazzling spark which told him that some one, somewhere, had something to say to him across the water and through the black, silent night.

Quickly he adjusted the receivers on his ears and waited. The clamorous buzzing sound caused the other operator to open his eyes and raise his sleepy head to his elbow.

Dash, dash, dash—dash, dot, dot, dot.

"What is it?" said the operator sleepily.

"Official business abbreviation," said Tom. "I'll take it—lie down."

It was no more than right that he should take it.

Hold Adolf von Stebel using passport Curry if on board. Tall, black mustache. Wanted for plotting and arson. New York.

"Huh!" said the chief operator sleepily. "Ring for a cabin boy and send it up to the bridge. Sign your own initials. G-good-night."

CHAPTER XXI

INTO THE DANGER ZONE

There was one part of the ship forbidden to passengers and all but forbidden to crew, where Archibald Archer disported and which was a spot of fascination to Tom in his numerous leisure hours. This was the railed-off stretch of deck astern where Billy Sunday and the gun crew held constant vigil. This enticing spot was irresistible to the ship's boys, and they lingered at the railing of the hallowed precinct, the bolder among them, such as Archer, making flank movements and sometimes grand drives through the rope fence, there to stand and chat until they were discovered by the second officer on his rounds.

The members of the gun crew who were not occupied in scanning the water with their glasses were glad enough to beguile the tedium of the days before the danger zone was reached in banter with these youngsters.

The next day after Tom's promotion Archibald Archer came running pell-mell to the wireless room where he was reading in the berth.

"A submarine! A submarine!" he shouted at the top of his voice. "Come ahead, Slady!"

The regular operator did not seem in the least concerned, but Tom, roused out of his usual calm, followed Archer up the steps and to the rope railing where several of the ship's boys were congregated.

"Let him see," commanded Archer.

Tommy Walters handed the marine glass to Tom. "Over there to the west," he said.

"It's just a periscope," said Archer. "See? See it sticking up?"

Looking far out over the water, Tom could see through the long glass a dark, thin upright object which seemed to move as he looked at it.

"O-o-oh, ye-e-es!" he exclaimed, gazing intently. "It's a periscope, sure!"

"Look over there to the west!" shouted Archer suddenly. "Is that another one?"

Tom turned the glass to the westward, and sure enough, there was another one.

"We're surrounded! There's a whole fleet of 'em! Oh, joy!" exclaimed Archer. "Look there to the south!"

Tom looked, and to his great excitement there was another periscope.

"Now turn the glass upside down," said Archer.

Tom did so, and perceived to his amazement that the periscope stuck out of the sky instead of out of the water.

By this time everybody was laughing, and Tommy Walters leaned against the gun, shaking with glee.

"Now look on the other end of the glass," said Archer, dodging behind a stanchion.

Tom, in bewilderment, obeyed, and pulled out a match-end.

"Tag; you're it," said Archer delightedly; "don't throw it away."

"Why not?" said Tom, laughing sheepishly.

"Because you have to wear it with a ribbon," said the irrepressible Archer, fastening it to Tom's buttonhole with a piece of baby ribbon. "You're easy, Slady!"

"I always was," said Tom.

"You should worry," laughed Walters. "They all have to stand for that."

When Tom got back to the wireless room, Cattell, the operator, looked at the badge with a knowing smile.

"Stung, eh?" said he. "I thought you were on to Archer by this time."

"It's always easy to jolly me," said Tom.

"That's an old trick," said Cattell. "Don't you know we won't be in the danger zone until Monday?"

"I never thought about that," said Tom.

"You're easy," laughed Cattell. "When we get into the Zone,

you'll know it."

And so Tom found, for early Monday morning, as he went along the deck on his way to breakfast, he noticed several persons wearing life preservers. They looked clumsy and ridiculous, and if the occasion had been less serious even Tom's soberness must have yielded at their funny appearance.

As he passed along he noticed members of the crew in the life-boats removing the canvas covers, and as these were taken off he could see that the boats were already stocked, each with a cask and a good-sized wooden case. A member of the crew patrolled the rope rail which shut off the guncrew's little domain, and no one could trespass there now. From a distance Tom could see Billy Sunday fully revealed without any vestige of canvas cover, and the boys in khaki scanning the waters in every direction with their glasses. All day long this continued, and once or twice when he met them hurrying along the deck they hardly recognized him.

Cattell, calm as usual, sat all day at the instrument shelf with the receivers on, and ate his luncheon there. Tom forsook his berth, where he was wont to spend his spare time reading, and remained close to the telephone where open connection was kept with the bridge.

It was a day of suspense. Ship's officers hurried back and forth with serious faces and looks of grave responsibility. Twice through the day the emergency drill was gone through, the boats occupied and vacated and the tackle tested, to the dismal voice of the megaphone on the bridge. And as night came on the more constant callings of the lookouts from their wind-swept perches and the answering call through the darkness had an ominous and portentous sound which shook even Tom's wonted stolidness and made him feel apprehensive and restless.

Not a light was there upon the ship as she plowed steadily upon her course, and little knots of people stood here and there in the darkness looking grotesquely ill-shapen in their cumbersome life-belts.

Along the deck, as he came back from supper, which had been served behind closed portholes and with but a single dim light, Tom met Mr. Conne sauntering along at his customary gait, with no sign of life-belt, but with his companionable cigar dimly visible in the darkness.

"H'lo, Tommy," said he cheerily.

Something, perhaps the tenseness which had gripped the spirits of all on board and affected even him, prompted him to pause for a moment's chat with Tom. He leaned against the rail in the black solitude, his easy manner in strange contrast to the portentous darkness and rising wind, and the general atmosphere of suspense.

"Where's your life-belt, Tommy?"

"I don't want to be bothered with one," said Tom. "I'll grab one if there's one handy when the time comes."

"Ain't you 'fraid old Uncle Neptune'll get you?"

"I've risked my life before this," said Tom; "I just as soon put one on, though," he added; "only I never thought about it."

"Hmmm," said Mr. Conne, looking at him sharply. "There was a fellow last trip put one on before we got outside Sandy Hook," he added.

"Why don't *you* wear one?" Tom asked.

"Me? Oh, I don't know—I don't think I look real well in a cork sash.... I bet you wouldn't have your photograph taken in one of those things," he added, after a moment's pause.

"Is Mr. von Stebel all right?" Tom ventured to ask.

"Oh, yes, he's all right; but glum as a rainy Sunday."

"Did he have any papers?" Tom asked, encouraged by the detective's agreeable manner.

"Well, he had a passport. Of course, it was forged. He had a trolley transfer from Wyndham, Ohio, 'bout a hundred miles west of Cleveland, and, let's see, a hotel bill of the Hotel Bishop in Cleveland. He has a suite there, I guess. I'd like to rummage through his trunk. I tripped him up two or three times, enough to find that he's got a lot of information about army places. Seems to have more of it in his head than he had in his pockets."

"You'll take him back, won't you?" Tom asked.

"Yes, or maybe send him back on the first ship across. They'll turn him inside out in New York. I don't believe he'll leave you anything in his will, Tommy."

Tom laughed. "It would be bad if he got to Germany, wouldn't it?" he asked. "I mean with all the information he's got."

"It would be worse than bad," said Mr. Conne. "It might be disastrous."

He moved on, clinging to the hand-rail along the stateroom

tier to steady himself, for the wind was rising to a gale and driving the sea in black mountains which burst in spray upon the deck, wetting Tom through and through as he scurried back to the wireless room for the night's long vigil.

CHAPTER XXII

SOS

Bzzz ... bzzz, bzzz, bzzz...... bzzz ... bz, bz, bz, bz ... bz ... ... bzzz, bz, bz ... bz, bzzz ... bzzz, bz, bzzz, bzzz.

"What is it?" Tom asked, standing in the doorway of the wireless room and looking at the black outline of Cattell's form as he sat at the instrument shelf. He could hardly see Cattell for the darkness. It seemed darker, even, than it did out on deck. Some small object fell, and the sound seemed emphasized by the darkness.

"Huh, there goes my paperweight again," said Cattell; "it's getting rough, isn't it?"

Tom groped around and found it; then, standing, grasped the door-jamb again.

"I had to grab the hand-rail coming along," he said; "do you want to turn in?"

"No; I couldn't sleep, anyway; I might as well be here."

"What was that you took?" Tom asked, as he clambered up into the berth and settled himself comfortably. He, too, could not sleep.

"Same old stuff," said Cattell; "*To the day*. They're drinking each other's health again."

"I got that a couple of times," said Tom; "what is it, anyway?"

Cattell reached out and pushed the door shut. "Must be pretty chizzly for those fellows up in the crow's-nest," he said.

"Yes; it's queer to hear them calling in the dark, isn't it?"

"You didn't see any lights in the stateroom ports as you came along, did you?" Cattell asked.

"Nope; there's a sailor marching back and forth outside along the starboard tier. Everything's as dark as pitch."

They were silent for a few minutes, listening to the rising wind and to the sound of the spray as it broke over the deck. Cattell folded a despatch blank and stuffed it in the crack of the door to stop its rattling.

"It's comfortable in here, anyway," said Tom; "it's kind of like camping."

Again there was silence, broken only by the wind outside and the occasional voice of the lookout, thin and spent as from another world, and the scarcely audible, long-drawn-out answer from the bridge.

"'To the day,'" said Cattell, sticking his feet upon the shelf, "means to the day the Kaiser will own the earth—emperor of the world. In the German navy, whenever they take a drink they always say, 'To the day.' The day that poor Austrian guy was murdered in Serbia—you know, that prince—and the Kaiser saw his chance to start the ball rolling, all the high dinkums in the German navy had a jambouree, and some old gink—von Somebody or other—said: 'Now, to the day.'"

"Well, it got to be a kind of password or slogan, as you might say. If a German spy wants to let another German know that he's all right, he uses a sentence with those three words in. And the sub-commanders are all the time slinging it around the ocean—testing their instruments sometimes, I dare say. It don't do any harm, I suppose. Talk's cheap."

"I wondered what it meant," said Tom.

"That's all it means. When you hear that you'll know some sub-captain is taking a drink of wine or something. When the *Emden* captured an English ship a couple of years ago, it happened there was a nice, gentlemanly German spy on board the Britisher. The German captain was just going to pack him off with the others as a prisoner when he said something with those three words in it. The German commander understood, and they didn't take any of his things, but just let him stay among the English, and the English weren't any the wiser."

"Huh," said Tom.

Again there was silence.

"I think the other operator is all right, don't you?" Tom asked.

"Sure—is or *was*. He may have been killed down there and thrown overboard. He was straight as a bee-line. You put Conne on the right track, all right."

"Do you think they'll ever find out about the rest of it?" Tom asked.

Cattell shrugged his shoulders. "Search *me*," he said.

All night long the wind blew and the swell broke noisily against the ship and beat over the rail. At intervals, when Tom climbed down and stumbled over to open the door for a glimpse of the sullen night, the slanting rain blew in his face, and he closed the door again with difficulty. It would have been a ticklish business to make one's way along the deck then, he thought.

It was a couple of hours before dawn, and Tom, lulled by the darkness, had fallen into a doze, when he was roused by a sudden shock and sat upright clutching the side of the berth.

"What is it?" he said. "Are you there, Cattell?"

Afterward, when he recalled that moment, and tried to describe the shock, he said it seemed as if the vessel were shaking herself, as a dog shakes himself. The crash, which he had so often read about, he did not hear at all; no sound except the heedless wind and the restless, beating sea. It merely seemed as if the mighty ship were cold and had shuddered.

"It ain't anything, is it?" he asked, nevertheless climbing down from his berth.

Then he became aware of something which startled him more than the shock had done. The steady throbbing which had been continuously present since that midnight when the ship first sailed, had ceased. The absolute stillness under his feet seemed strange and ominous.

"It ain't—anything wrong—is it?" he repeated.

"I think we're struck," said Cattell quietly.

For a moment Tom breathed heavily, standing just where he was.

"Can I turn on the light?" he asked. The groping darkness seemed to unnerve him more than anything else now—that and the awful stillness under his feet.

"No—put the flashlight on the clock and see what time it is."

There were sounds outside now, and amid them the doleful distant voice of the megaphone.

"Not three yet," said Tom.... "You—you sending out the call?"

"Yup."

A man in oilskins, carrying a lantern, threw open the door. The rain was streaming from his garments and his hat.

"We're struck amidships," he said.

The telephone from the bridge rang.

"Answer that; find out where we are," said Cattell.

As Tom repeated the latitude and longitude the urgent "S O S" went forth into the night. Lights were now visible outside, and the emergency gong could be heard ringing, mingled with the hollow, far-off voice of the megaphone.

"Better beat it to your post," said Cattell calmly, as his finger played the key. "I'll take care of this." He did not seem at all excited, and his quiet manner gave Tom self-control.

He went out and along the deck where the drenching rain glistened in the fresh glare of the lights. Once, twice, he slipped and went sprawling to the rail. He wondered whether it was from the roughness of the sea or because the vessel was tilting over.

All about hurried people with life preservers on, some sprawling on the deck like himself, in their haste. One man said the ship had been struck above the waterline and would float. Others said she was settling; others that she was sinking fast.

Tom's emergency post was at port davits P 27 on the promenade deck. He knew what to do, for he had gone through the emergency drill twice a day, but the tumultuous sea and the darkness and the cold, driving rain disconcerted him.

Reaching the rail by the life-boat davits, he saw at once that the ship was canting far over. The life-boat, which in the drills swung close to the vessel's side, now hung far away. It was already filled and being lowered.

Falling in line with several of the crew, Tom grasped the rope, and was surprised at the ease with which the boat was lowered by means of the multiplied leverage of the block and falls. In the drills, they had manned but never lowered the boats.

"Don't try that," some one called from the descending boat. "You can't make it, and we're crowded." The voice sounded strangely clear. "Better go up on deck," another voice said.

Tom thought that some one must be trying to reach the descending boat from one of the portholes below.

Then the rope slackened and an officer called, "All right?"

"All right," some one answered; "but she can't ride this."

Tom pressed close to the rail and looked down through the blinding rain. He could see only dark figures and a lantern bobbing frantically.

"Pull her round crossways to the swell and get away from the side—quick!" the officer in charge called.

"She's half full of water," answered a voice amid the wind and storm.

Men came rushing from the starboard deck where they said the boats could not be launched because of the angle of the ship's side which prevented them from swinging free. They were obedient enough, but greatly alarmed when told that they must wait their turn.

The few army men on board were models of efficiency and quiet discipline, herding back the excited passengers and trying to keep them away from the rail, for the slant of the deck was now almost perpendicular.

"Help those people launch that hatch if they want to," said an officer to Tom.

Acting on the suggestion, a dozen or more men ranged themselves around the hatch and Tom helped to lift it, while others clustered about, ready to climb upon it.

"You'll have to clear away from here," said an officer;

Percy K. Fitzhugh

"sixteen is the limit for one of those hatches. There are seven more." Evidently the rescuing capacity of the hatches had already been ascertained.

The frightened people hurried along through the driving rain and the darkness, some of them slipping on the streaming deck and sliding pell-mell to the rail, which broke away with the impact in one place and precipitated several screaming persons into the ocean.

Hurriedly Tom counted those around the hatch and found that the officer had evidently included him among the sixteen who should man it.

"Do you mean for me to go too?" he asked, in his usual dull manner.

"You might as well," the officer answered brusquely.

The great vessel had lost all its pride and dignity, and seemed a poor, reeling, spiritless thing. The deck was deserted save for the little group about the hatch who strove with might and main to launch this last poor medium of rescue. The abrupt pitch of the deck made their frantic efforts seem all but hopeless, and walking, even standing, was quite out of the question. Tom could feel the ship heeling over beneath him.

Even the cheerily authoritative voice of the megaphone up on the bridge had now ceased, and there was no reassuring reminder of life there—nothing but the black outline of the trestled structure, slanting at a dreadful angle with the water pouring from it.

Tom and his distracted companions were evidently the last on board.

The rail was now so low that the plunge of the hatch would not be very hazardous at all events, for the seething waters beat over the deck now and again, rolling up as on a beach at the seashore and adding their ominous chill to Tom's already chilled body.

Out of the turmoil of the sea sounds rose, some the even tones of command, sounding strangely out of place in the storm; others which he recognized with a shudder as the last frightful gasps of drowning persons.

In a minute—two minutes—he would be plunged into that seething brine where he still might hear but could not see. Instinctively he increased his exertions with this makeshift raft which, if they could but cling to it till the sea subsided, might bear them up until succor came.

As soon as the hatch was raised, it began to slide away, and those who had lifted it jumped upon it, clinging as best they could.

From somewhere out of the darkness a man came rushing pell-mell for this precarious refuge. As he jumped upon it, clutching frantically at the moulding around its edge, Tom stepped off.

The angle of the careening ship was now so steep that he could not stand upon the deck, but as he slipped he caught hold of a vent pipe and so managed to reach the stateroom tier where all the doors hung open like the covers of so many inverted cigar boxes, flapping in the wind and rain.

The hatch had slid to the deck's edge and was held precariously by the doubtful strength of the straining rail.

"Get on!" one of the men called to Tom. "Hurry up!"

Percy K. Fitzhugh

"The officer said only sixteen," he answered.

"Are you crazy?" another man called. "Get on while you can!"

"He said only sixteen," Tom called back impassively.

"It's every man for himself now and no orders!" shouted another. Perhaps it was the man who had usurped Tom's place.

"He said only—"

The rest of his answer was drowned by the crashing of the rail as the hatch went plunging from the deck into the black turmoil below. The last they saw of him, he was clinging to one of the flapping doors, his foot braced against a cable cleat, his shock of hair blowing wildly this way and that, the rain streaming from his face and soaking clothes.

He did not look at all like a hero, nor even like the picture of a scout on the cover of a boys' magazine....

CHAPTER XXIII

ROY BLAKELEY KEEPS STILL—FOR A WONDER

"Yes, that was the one trouble with Tom Slade—he couldn't obey orders."

"I think you're rather severe," said Mrs. Ellsworth.

"He had his work all cut out for him here," persisted her husband relentlessly. "He knew the part the scouts were supposed to play in the war, but he thought he knew more than I did about it. He gave me his promise, and then he broke his word. He flunked on his first duty."

Mr. Ellsworth pushed his coffee cup from him and pushed his chair back from the dining table in a very conclusive manner.

For a moment no one spoke. The young man in the soldier's uniform gazed into his empty cup and said nothing. Then he looked up at Mrs. Ellsworth as if he hoped she would answer her husband. Of the four who sat there in the Ellsworths' pleasant little dining room, Roy Blakeley was the first to speak.

"He'll make a good soldier, anyway," he said.

Percy K. Fitzhugh

"A good soldier is one who obeys orders," said Mr. Ellsworth, tightening his lips uncompromisingly. "Tom Slade's war duties were very clearly mapped out for him. And, besides, he gave me his promise; you heard him, didn't you?"

"Yes, I did," said Roy reluctantly.

"All I asked of him," continued the scoutmaster, "was to do his bit as a scout with the Colors, till he was of military age. He gave me his promise—you heard him—and then he desert—"

"Oh, don't say that," said Mrs. Ellsworth; "that's a dreadful word!"

The young man in uniform bit his lip and started to move his chair back; then, as if uncertain what to do, remained where he was.

"A promise is a promise," said the scoutmaster. "You can't build up anything good on the foundation of a broken promise."

"Don't you think a person *might* be justified in breaking a promise?" said the soldier diffidently.

"No, sir; not if it is humanly possible to keep it.—Besides, Tom must have had to lie to get into the army."

There was a moment's pause.

"It was dreadful to think of his pawning his Gold Cross," said Mrs. Ellsworth; "if he had only kept his word and waited a little while—"

"He would never have had that Cross to pawn if he hadn't

been brave," said Roy, flushing slightly.

"Good for you, Roy!" said the young soldier.

Mr. Ellsworth laughed pleasantly at Roy's unshakable faith in his absent friend.

"That's right, Roy," said Mrs. Ellsworth, with a very sweet smile. "You stand up for him."

"If I can't stand up for him, I'll keep still," said Roy.

"Well, then, I guess you'll have to keep still," laughed Mr. Ellsworth, "for there isn't much defense. I did all I could for Tom," he added, more soberly. "If his three years of scouting didn't teach him to keep his word with me as I always kept mine with him, it must have been to no purpose. He might have waited a little, kept his solemn promise, and gone into the army under the same honorable conditions as you did," he said, turning to the soldier; "and we should all have—"

"What's the matter?" exclaimed Roy.

Roscoe Bent had thrown his chair back and without so much as excusing himself had stridden over to the bay window, where he stood holding the curtain aside and looking out.

"What is it—reveille?" the scoutmaster laughed.

"May I smoke a cigarette?" Roscoe asked nervously.

"Uncle Sam hasn't cured you of that, has he?" Mr. Ellsworth laughed. "Sure; go ahead."

The soldier's abrupt movement seemed to terminate the little after-dinner chat, and Mrs. Ellsworth, bent on other duties perhaps, or possibly foreseeing that her husband wished to "talk business," arose also and left the three to themselves.

"I—er—don't smoke as much as I did," said Roscoe; "but sometimes—er—a cigarette sort of pulls you together. What—what were you going to say?"

He returned and sat down again at the table.

"Why, nothing in particular," said Mr. Ellsworth, "except this: I want you to drive home to these boys of mine this lesson of obedience, this necessity for respecting a promise above all things, and of obeying an order from one whom they've promised to obey. You get me?"

"I—I think I do."

"This meeting which we're holding in conjunction with the Y. M. C. A. to-morrow night is the last one before I go away myself. When I heard you were going to be home from camp over the week-end, it just popped into my head that I'd ask you to come around and give the boys a spiel. They've all got a great admiration for you, Roscoe. I suppose it's because your uniform becomes you so well. You make a pretty fine-looking soldier. Anybody tell you that?"

"Miss—Margaret Ellison, in the Temple Camp office, was kind enough to hint as much," admitted Roscoe humorously.

He did look pretty handsome in his new khaki. He had a figure as straight as an arrow and a way of holding his head and carrying himself with the true soldier air. Besides, his blond, wavy hair, always attractive, seemed to harmonize with his brown uniform, and his blue eyes had a kind of dancing recklessness in them.

"All the boys have promised to be there—the Methodist Troop, the East Bridgeboro Troop, and mine—"

"Which is the best of all," put in Roy.

Roscoe laughed merrily.

"We'll have the Y. M. C. A. boys and three full troops as well."

"Except for Tom," said Roy.

"We won't talk of Tom any more," said Mr. Ellsworth. "That's a tale that is told. It's a closed book."

"It isn't with me," said Roy bravely.

"I want you to tell the boys—there'll be some girls there, too, if they want to come—"

"Oh, joy!" Roy commented.

"I'm glad to see you bucking up," said the scoutmaster. "I want you to tell the boys," he went on to Roscoe, "a little about life down in Camp Dix. Tell them how you enlisted."

"I didn't enlist—I was drafted."

"Well, it's much the same—you were glad to be drafted. There were a whole lot of you fellows who didn't get around to enlisting who were glad enough when the call came. You didn't need any urging, I'll bet."

"N-no," said Roscoe.

"And so I want you to tell these scouts, just in your own

way, what it means to be a soldier. Dwell on the sense of honor which this fine military discipline gives. Tell them what is meant by a parole, and what it means to break a parole—which is just breaking your promise. I don't care so much about the guns and swords just now—I mean as far as to-morrow night is concerned. But I'd like these scouts to know that there's something besides fighting to being a soldier—a real one. I'd like them to know that a soldier's word can be trusted, his promise depended on. If anything that has happened in my troop," he added significantly, "has given them a wrong impression—you correct that impression. See?"

"I'll try to."

"That's it. You know, Roscoe, most boys, and some scouts even, think that a soldier is just a fellow who shoots and makes raids and storms fortifications and all that. There's many a boy thinks he can be a soldier by just running off to the war. But that's where he's got a couple of more thinks coming, as Roy here would say. Uncle Sam wants soldiers, but he doesn't want to be lied to and cheated—"

Roy winced.

"I want you to give them just a little off-hand, heart-to-heart talk about the other end of it—how a 'soldier's wealth is honor,' as old What's-his-name, the poet, says."

"I'll try to," said Roscoe.

"Then there's another thing. I'm off with the engineering corps myself pretty soon. And my three patrols are going to feel pretty bad to see me go, too. That so, Roy?"

"You bet it is," said Roy.

"Tell them they ought to be proud to see me go. They'll listen to you, because you're a regular A-One, all-around soldier, you're nearer to their own age, and you're an outsider. Tell them how tickled you were to get your name down on that little old roll of honor—"

Roscoe rose suddenly.

"Don't—please don't," said he.

"What's the matter?" Mr. Ellsworth asked.

"Nothing—only—I have to go home now. I—I understand, and I'll do it—I'll—I'm not much on speechmaking, but I know what you mean, and—"

"That's right, you get the idea," Mr. Ellsworth exclaimed, rising and slapping him on the shoulder. "I won't keep you any later, for I know they're waiting for you around in Rockwood Place."

"I'll only have this one night at home," said Roscoe.

"And I'll bet they're proud of you round there, too," Mr. Ellsworth added, as he followed them into the front hall. "I've got three full patrols—that is, two, I mean; and Connie Bennett expects to dig up another boy for us. Roy refused the job. Never had a kid of my own, but I'd like to have a soldier boy like you."

He helped Roscoe on with his big army ulster, and stood with a hand on either of Roscoe's shoulders.

"You tell your father when you get home that I congratulate him. Providence did him a good turn, as we scouts say."

"I dare say somebody or other did him a good turn," said Roscoe, almost in a tone of disgust.

"Tell him I said he ought to be proud to furnish Uncle Sam with such a soldier."

"Humph," said Roscoe, in the same mood; "it's a question who furnished Uncle Sam with the soldier."

"What do you mean?" asked Mr. Ellsworth, slightly puzzled.

"Oh, nothing in particular—I guess. I'm kind of tired—I'll be—glad when I get in bed...."

CHAPTER XXIV

A SOLDIER'S HONOR

As the two walked along the dark street together, Roscoe, in his long military coat, seemed taller than he really was and the boy at his side seemed small and young to him.

He knew Roy only as everybody in a small city knows everybody else, but Roy knew Roscoe as every boy in Bridgeboro knew the soldiers whom the town had given to the Colors. He was proud to have been at that little supper party, and he was proud now to be walking along at Roscoe's side.

"Gee, I'd like to come down to Camp Dix!" he said.

"Pretty hard for outsiders to get in the place now," said Roscoe, "unless you're a wife, a mother, or a sweetheart."

"I'm only a boy sprout," said Roy, his wonted buoyancy persisting. "I wouldn't go where I'm not welcome.... They might think I was a German spy, hey?"

Roscoe looked down at him and laughed. Roy amused him, and he felt a little twinge of sympathy for him, too.

Percy K. Fitzhugh

"Ellsworth's pretty strict, isn't he?" he said. "I mean sort of—he's got pretty strict ideas," he added, anxious not to say too much in criticism.

Roy was silent for a moment. Then he said: "Gee, I hate to see that vacant place in the Elk Patrol filled up! I know a lot of fellows who'd be glad to come in, but I just can't ask them. That's what he meant when he said I wouldn't take the job. Maybe you don't understand what I mean, but as long as that place isn't filled, it seems like a—kind of as if it was in memory of Tom—as you might say. It's a crazy idea, I suppose."

Roscoe looked at him marching along with his scout hat set jauntily on the back of his curly head in a way that was characteristic of him.

"I don't see anything crazy about it," he said.

"A lot of fellows always said Tom was kind of crazy, anyway," Roy concluded; "but you can be crazy in a good way—can't you?"

"Yes, you bet!"

"If I only knew where he was," said Roy, with a little catch in his voice, "it wouldn't seem so bad."

"If I knew where he is, I'd tell you," said Roscoe simply.

"How could *you* know? You never even knew him. Even Mr. Ellsworth didn't know him the way I did."

"Oh, yes, I knew him," said Roscoe; "not as well as you did, of course; but I'll tell you this much, kiddo: I don't believe he lied to any one, and I don't believe he broke his promise."

"Honest, don't you?"

"No, I don't."

"I wish—I wish you had told Mr. Ellsworth that."

"I couldn't have proved—I mean—well, it isn't so easy to talk to Mr. Ellsworth as it is to you, kiddo."

"I'll tell you something if you'll promise not to tell it—not even to Mr. Ellsworth," said Roy.

"A soldier's word of honor," said Roscoe, with a little bitter sneer.

"All the fellows in the Elk Patrol—that's Tom's own patrol, he started it—they made an agreement they wouldn't ask any fellows to join, or even vote for one—not for six months. In that time we might hear something—you can't tell. Mr. Ellsworth may possibly be wrong. Something may have happened to Tom. My patrol and the Ravens, they mostly agree with Mr. Ellsworth, and even some of the Elks do, I guess; but I asked them as a special favor."

"So they're doing it for your sake, eh?"

"Yop. And oh, gee, I'm glad you're with me! I didn't know you ever knew Tom Slade.—I'm glad you think the way I do.—I used to see you with Rolf Brownell in his automobile. I didn't know who you were then.... I—I believe in sticking to a fellow through thick and thin—don't you?"

"Some fellows."

"I got Tom in the troop, you know."

"You did a good job, I guess, that time," said Roscoe absently.

"You can bet I did.—Cracky, I'm awful anxious to hear you to-morrow night. You'll get a lot of applause—from me; that's dead sure!"

Roscoe laughed. He had an engaging laugh.

"It seems as if you're sort of an ally now," said Roy. "There aren't any of the troop that really agree with me," he added dubiously. "Well, here's where I have to leave you. Don't forget to tell your father what Mr. Ellsworth said."

Roscoe laughed shortly.

"About supplying Uncle Sam with a good soldier, you know."

They paused at the corner.

"You can't always tell who really does the supplying, kiddo.—It might possibly be a fellow's mother, say—or a girl—or—"

"I bet girls like you, all right. And I bet you're brave too. Gee, you must have felt proud on Registration Day when you stood in line to register. I bet you were one of the first ones, weren't you? We helped that day, too. Maybe you saw me—I gave out badges. But I guess you wouldn't remember because you were probably all—all thrilled; you know what I mean. That was the day—Tom—didn't show up—"

Roscoe Bent walked on alone. In a drug store window on the opposite corner was a placard, the handiwork of the scouts, which showed how much store Mr. Ellsworth set on the meeting of the next night:

SPECIAL! SPECIAL!

and a little farther down:

SCOUT GAMES EXHIBITIONS OF SCOUT SKILL
AND RESOURCE

and so forth, and so forth:

ONE OF OUR OWN BOYS FROM CAMP DIX,
PRIVATE ROSCOE BENT, WILL TELL OF SOLDIER
LIFE. COME AND GIVE HIM A WELCOME

There was more, but that was all Roscoe saw. It sickened
him to read it. He went on, heavy hearted, trying to comfort
himself with the reflection that he really did not know where
Tom was or what he was doing. But it did not afford him
much comfort.

As he walked along, his head down, certain phrases ran
continually through his mind. They came out of the past, like
things dead, out of another life which Roscoe Bent knew no
more: *Do you think I'd let them get you? Do you think
because you made fun of me ... I wouldn't be a friend to you?
I got the strength to strangle you! I know the trail—I'm a
scout—and I got here first. They'd have to kill me to make me
tell....*

Roscoe Bent looked behind him, as if he expected to see
some one there. But there was nothing but the straight, long
street, in narrowing perspective.

Under a lamp post on the next corner he took out of his
alligator-skin wallet a folded paper, very much worn on the

creases, and holding it so that the light caught it he skimmed hurriedly the few half-legible sentences:

"... glad you didn't tell. If you had told it would have spoiled it all—so I'm going to help the government in a way I can do without lying to anybody.... can see I'm not the kind that tells lies. The thing ... most glad about ... that you got registered. ... like you and I always did, even when you made fun of me."

"*I* made fun—" he mumbled, crumpling the letter and sticking it into the capacious pocket of Uncle Sam's big coat. "*I*—Christopher! If I only had your nerve now—Tommy. It doesn't—it doesn't count for so much to be able to strangle a fellow—though I ought to be strangled.—It's just like Margaret said—the other kind of strength. If I could only make up my mind to do a thing, like he could, and *then do it*!"

He leaned against the lamp post, this fine young soldier who was going to help "can the Kaiser," and he did not stand erect at all, and all his fine air was gone from him.

You had better not slink and slouch like that on the platform to-morrow night, Private Roscoe Bent.

"I can see myself giving my father that message! Proud of me—of *me! Brave soldier!* That's what this poor kid said. And me trying to flim-flam myself into thinking that I've got to keep still because I promised Tom. How is it any of his business? It's between me and my—And I made fun of him—*him!* I wonder what this bully scout kid would say to that! I'm—I'm a low-down, contemptible sneak—that's what—"

On a sudden impulse, the same fine impulse which would

some day carry him ahead of his comrades, straight across the German trenches, he ran to the corner where he had parted with Roy and looked eagerly up one street and down another. He ran to the next corner and looked anxiously down the street which crossed there. He ran a block up this street and looked as far as he could see along Terrace Place which was the way up to the fine old Blakeley homestead on the hill.

But no sign of Roy was there to be seen, for the good and sufficient reason that when Roy Blakeley, "Silver Fox," took it into his head to go scout pace, he was presently invisible to pursuers.

So Roscoe's impulse passed, as Roscoe's impulses were very apt to do, and he wandered homeward, telling himself that fate had been against him and balked his noble resolution.

As he went down through Rockwood Place he saw the lights in the library, which told him that his mother and father were still up. But he did not deliver Mr. Ellsworth's message; he was strong enough for that, anyway. Instead, he went straight up to his own room, which he had not occupied lately, and when he got up there he found that he was not alone. For a certain face haunted him all night and would not go away—a face with a heavy shock of hair, with a big, rugged mouth, and a bloody cut on its forehead.

CHAPTER XXV

THE FACE

All the next day that face haunted Roscoe. "If I could only know where he is," he said to himself; "if I could bring him back, I'd tell the whole business."

It occurred to him that perhaps Tom was dead and that that was why he was continually seeing that stolid face with the bloody scar. "Maybe the cut got worse and he got blood poisoning and died," he thought.

This train of thought possessed him so that he grew to believe that Tom Slade must really be dead. And that being the case, there would be no use in telling anybody anything....

At breakfast he seemed so preoccupied that after he left the room his mother said to his father,

"You don't think he's nervous or timid, do you?"

"I think he's a little nervous about making a speech in public," said Mr. Bent. "He isn't afraid of anything else," he added proudly.

During the morning Mrs. Bent wanted to take his picture. "You look so splendid and handsome in your uniform, dear!" she told him. So he stood in the big bay window where the sunlight streamed in and let her snap the camera at him. He did look splendid and handsome, there was no denying that.

Then she would have him develop the film with his own hands so that she could make some prints right away. "You may not have another leave," she said. "It's dreadful that you have to go back to camp late to-night."

"Don't you care," he laughed, in that companionable way in which he always talked with his mother.

"You can take one of the prints over to East Bridgeboro to-night," she added, as an inducement to his developing the film at once.

"Think she'd like to have one?"

"The idea! Of course she would."

So, to please his mother, Roscoe took off Uncle Sam's service coat, put on a kitchen apron, and went into his little familiar dark closet to wrestle with chemicals.

And there again, in the dim light of the red lantern, and the deathlike quiet, he saw that face—with the cut and the thick, disordered hair, and the big, tight-set mouth. "You can see yourself it wouldn't do for anybody to know," he fancied the lips saying. "If you told, it would spoil it all—"

"I won't spoil it," Roscoe mumbled, as if he were doing the shadowy presence a great favor.

Private Bent, who was going to "can the Kaiser," was glad to

Percy K. Fitzhugh

get out of that dark, stuffy place.

In the afternoon he went down into the cellar to grease and cover up his motorcycle in anticipation of his long absence "over there." This would be his last chance to do it, unless he got up very early in the morning. But then he would be an hour over his leave in getting back to camp late to-night on a milk train. A soldier's honor must not be sullied by a stolen hour....

And there again Roscoe Bent saw that face. It was a little more than a face this time. He could almost have sworn that he saw the figure of Tom Slade standing over in the dark corner near the coal bins; and as Roscoe, kneeling by his motorcycle, fixed his eyes upon this thing another sentence ran through his thoughts: "Those secret service fellows—do yer think I'd let them get yer? Do you think because you made fun of me...."

He tried to stare the apparition down, but it would not disappear—not until he went over to it and saw that it was just a burlap bag full of kindling wood, with James, the furnace man's, old felt hat thrown upon it.

"I—I know what it means, all right," he muttered; "it means he's dead."

After supper he parted his wavy blond hair, and his mother brushed his uniform while he stood straight as an arrow, his handsome head thrown back. Then his father proudly helped him into his big military coat and he started for East Bridgeboro, which was across the river. The new Y. M. C. A. hall was not over there, but he was going there first, just the same.

"Have you got the print?" his mother called after him.

"Sure."

"The one holding the gun? You look so soldierly and brave in that!"

He laughed as he went down the steps.

But presently he became moody and preoccupied again. "If Mr. Ellsworth hadn't dragged me into this thing," he said to himself, "it wouldn't be so bad. It gets my goat to stand up there and shoot off about honor and all that sort of thing. But I can't do anything else now. I'm not going to spoil it all. It can't make any difference to Tom now—he's out of the game. He's through with the scouts, and he's through with Bridgeboro—dead, I'm afraid. And if I just keep my mouth shut, it'll be doing just what he wanted me to do; it was *his* idea."

So that was settled; and in place of those troubling thoughts, Roy Blakeley bobbed up in his mind—Roy Blakeley, who believed in "standing by a fellow through thick and thin"; who was staunch and loyal to his friend.

"He's a bully kid," mused Roscoe, as he crossed the bridge whence the town derived its name, and the more he thought about Roy the more mean and contemptible he felt himself to be.

At the scouts' float hard by the bridge, the troop's cabin launch, the *Good Turn*, participant in many adventures, past and to come, lay moored.

Even the sophisticated Roscoe, who had never "bothered much with the kids," knew of this famous boat. There had been a photograph of it hanging in the Temple Camp office, with the face of Tom Slade peering out through the little

Percy K. Fitzhugh

hatchway. The sudden knocking of the hull against the float in the still night startled him, and as he looked down upon the moon-lit river with its black background of trees he fancied again that he saw the face of Tom Slade looking out from the hatchway of the boat.

"Hello, there!" he called, though of course he knew no one was there.

Once over the bridge, he took a short cut through Morrell's Grove for the River Road.

"It's best to let well enough alone," he told himself; "what's past is past. I'm not going to worry about it now. If Ellsworth hadn't hauled me into this thing, and given me that spiel, I wouldn't be bothering my head about things that happened months ago. I'm not going to worry."

He was singularly moody and dissatisfied for a person who was not going to worry.

"Wish I could get that Blakeley kid out of my head," he reflected.

But he couldn't exactly get that Blakeley kid out of his head, and he couldn't get that face out of his mind, nor Mr. Ellsworth's stinging words out of his memory. So he stumbled along through the dark grove, thinking what he should say to the boys and how he should talk to Margaret Ellison so as not to let her suspect his troubled conscience and general feeling of—not exactly meanness and dishonor, but....

"Girls are such blamed fiends for reading your thoughts," he grumbled.

About halfway through the grove he stopped suddenly in the narrow path. For there was that face again peering out of the darkness. There was a slouch hat on it this time, but the old familiar shock of hair protruded from under it and there was an ugly scar on the forehead.

"It's blamed dark in here," said Roscoe, as he pulled himself together. A lonely owl answered with a dismal shriek from a distant tree, making the night seem still more spooky.

Roscoe tried to whistle to keep up his spirits, but as he walked on along the path the face, instead of fading away, seemed to become clearer, and he could have sworn that there was the dark outline of a form below it leaning against a tree. It was only his fancy enlivened by his conscience, he knew, but it took him back to a night months before, when he had stood in a remote mountain trail and watched a figure clinging to a tree, and he remembered how he had stood speechless and listened, as a man may watch a thunderstorm. No one in all the wide world but those two had known of that meeting.

"Or ever will," thought Private Bent.

Suddenly he paused again, and he, Private Roscoe Bent, who would take delight in canning the Kaiser, who would give his young life if need be, to make the world free for democracy, trembled like a leaf.

The figure had moved—he was sure of it. For a couple of seconds he could not speak, he was breathing so heavily.

"Hello!" he finally managed to call.

"Hello!" came a dull voice. "There ain't any need to be afraid," it added. "*I* couldn't hurt you. I can't see very good—

　　　　Percy K. Fitzhugh

is—it—you—Roscoe?"

Roscoe spoke not a word but went forward and cautiously felt of the figure, laid his hand on the heavy thick shoulder and peered into the face.

"Tom Slade," he muttered.

"I didn't know you in your soldier's coat," said Tom; "it makes you look so tall and straight and—brave—"

Still the soldier did not speak, only kept his hand upon Tom's shoulder and looked into his square ugly face. And again the ghostly hoot of the owl made the little patch of woods seem more spooky and lonesome.

Then Private Roscoe Bent, Second Infantry, U. S. A., who intended to help roll the Teuton lines back and smash militarism once and for all, who would go over the top with all the fine frenzy of his impulsive nature and send the blond beast reeling, slipped his arm farther over Tom's shoulder until Tom Slade could feel the warmth from the thick sleeve of Uncle Sam's big military coat upon his own bare neck and threadbare flannel shirt. And the handsome head with its wavy blond hair which Private Roscoe Bent knew how to hold with such a fine air, hung down against that threadbare shirt in anything but martial fashion.

"Oh, Tom—Tom Slade—" he said, a feeling of great relief taking possession of him. "I know what to do now—now I can *see straight*—as you used to say.—You've come—to show me the right way, just as you did before."

CHAPTER XXVI

ROSCOE BENT BREAKS HIS PROMISE

"There ain't so much more to tell," said Tom, in his old lifeless way. "After that we got torpedoed. The officer said only sixteen could get on a raft, and there was a man who was anxious to get on and he made seventeen, so I got off. I guess I was the last one on the ship. She made an awful noise when she went down."

"Yes—and—"

"There's nothing else." Tom's reports of thrilling happenings were always provokingly tame and brief. "I swam around for about two hours, I guess. I had a piece of a door to hold on to. That scar's where a big wave banged me against it.—A schooner picked me up. I'd 'a' got picked up sooner, maybe, only I was the last one and I drifted away from the ship lane—sort of. It was going to South America after bananas, so they took me there."

"How'd you get back?"

"Came home on another ship. I worked cabin boy. They caught a German spy on the first ship."

It was quite like him not to tell how they *happened* to catch the spy.

"And then you came right here?"

"They gave me dinner in the Sailors' Mission in New York, and then I started out here."

"You don't mean you *walked*?"

"I'm going to Mrs. O'Connor's in the Alley where I used to live—till I can get a job. I made two good friends, but I don't know whether they were drowned.—You look good in your soldier suit."

Roscoe had to get control of himself before he could answer.

"That's a screech-owl," said Tom; "hear him? When you get —when I was a scout we had to learn the calls of all the different birds."

"Never mind that. Why did you go on that ship?"

"I told you—I wanted to help with the Colors."

Roscoe struggled again with his voice.

"Don't you think you did enough for the Colors," he said thickly, "when you gave me this uniform? Don't you think that was enough?"

"I didn't give it to you."

"Sit down here a minute. Don't you think you did enough for the Colors when you started me—over the top? Don't you?"

"It wasn't me. Anyhow, you can't do too much for the Colors."

Roscoe paused with his hand on Tom's knee. "No, I guess you can't," he said.

"You never told anybody, did you?" Tom asked.

"No," said Roscoe, with that little sneer of self-disgust. "I never told."

"It would of spoiled it all if you had. You got to be careful never to tell. You got to be specially careful, now you're a soldier—and look so fine and straight."

"Don't, Tom."

"You got to promise you'll never tell," said Tom, scenting danger in Roscoe's manner. "Will you?"

"Have you got any money at all, Tom?"

"You got to promise you'll never let 'em know about it now. Do you?"

"Never mind that, Tom—"

"You've got to. Do you?" Tom persisted.

"Can't you trust to a soldier's honor, Tom, without pinning him down?"

"Do you promise?"

"Won't you trust a friend? Won't you trust a soldier's honor, Tom?"

Percy K. Fitzhugh

"Yes," said Tom. "I will."

For a few moments Roscoe sat breathing audibly and staring at Tom as if hardly knowing what to do or say next.

"Do you know where I'm going now?" he asked, feeling the necessity of speaking.

"Maybe I could guess," said Tom: "you're going up River Road. I bet she said you looked fine in your uniform."

"Yes, I'm going there. I'm going to take her to a racket in Bridgeboro."

"It's funny how I met you here," said Tom.

"You walked all the way out on the turnpike road, I suppose. Tom," he broke off suddenly, "there isn't any time to sit here and talk now; listen. It seems as if all these weeks had been wiped out and we were back up on that mountain again."

"I knew you'd like it up there; I—"

"Never mind that; listen. We're back just where we were that night. We can make everything all right."

"Everything *is* all right."

"No, it isn't; everything *isn't* all right—old man. Tom, there's a meeting to-night, a sort of jumble—Y. M. C. A., scouts, and I don't know what all. Ellsworth nailed me for it. I've got to give the bunch a little spiel.—Tom, I want you to come to it—"

"I—"

"Now, don't start that; listen. It's in the new Y. M. C. A. Hall. I know you haven't got any clothes, if that's what you want to say, and I don't care a hang about your clothes. I don't ask you to blow in with the rest of them and sit in the audience," he went on hurriedly. "But just stroll around after everything's started and the lights are down. They couldn't see you—they won't notice you. Just stand in back."

"They got no use for me; they—"

"This is between you and me, old man; nobody else has got anything to do with it. Go down to Mrs. What's-her-name's—"

"O'Connor's," said Tom.

"Go down there and wash up, if you want to—I don't care. Only promise me you'll come around. I want you to see me make a show of myself. You'll have a good laugh—you old grouch," he added, with sudden good humor, "and after it's over we'll go up to my house and have a good long talk."

"I've often passed your house," said Tom.

"I'm going down to camp on a milk train about two A. M. This may be the last chance for us to see each other," Roscoe still spoke hurriedly; "they're sending troops across every week, Tom."

"I know they are."

"When I left you up on that mountain, Tom, I promised to come right back and register; and I did it, didn't I?"

"I told you nobody'd ever find out about that—"

"Never mind that. Will you do something for *me* now? Will you say you'll come?"

Tom hesitated. "I always said you'd be good at making speeches, and that kind of thing, but—'

Roscoe thrust his hand straight out. "Give me your hand, Tom, and say you'll come."

"Maybe I will."

"Say you'll come."

"I'd only stand in back after they put the lights down."

"Say you'll come," Roscoe persisted.

"All right."

"Sure, now?"

"I ain't the kind that breaks my word," said Tom dully. "But besides that, I want to hear you."

Roscoe held his hand tight for a full minute. Then they parted and he hurried along the River Road.

He was already late, but he would probably have hurried anyway, for when the heart is dancing it is hard for the feet to move slowly. And Roscoe's heart was dancing. He could "see straight" now, all right. To be a soldier you must see straight as well as shoot straight.

He swung along the River Road with a fine air, as if he owned it, and passing a small boy (bound across the river, perhaps) he lifted the youngster's hat off and handed it to him with a laugh. When he reached the Ellison cottage he deliberately kept pushing the bell button again and again, just out of sheer exuberance, until Margaret herself threw the door open and exclaimed,

"What in the world is the matter?"

"Nothing; can't you take a joke?"

"You're late," she said.

"Sure; I'm a punk soldier. That's a swell hat you've got on. Can you hustle? If you don't mind, we'll take the short cut through the grove."

It *was* a swell hat, there is no denying that, and she looked very pretty in it.

"I'm taking my knitting," she said, handing him one of those sumptuous bags with two vicious-looking knitting needles sticking out of it.

"I hate to go through the grove, it's so spooky," she said, as they hurried along. "I'm always seeing things there. Do you, ever?"

"Oh, yes."

"Really? What?"

"Oh, lions and tigers and things."

"Now you make me afraid," she shuddered.

"I met a lion in there to-night," he said; "that's what delayed me. If I see another one, I'll jab him with one of these knitting needles. Hear that screech-owl? He sounds like the Kaiser'll feel next year.—Do you know that Blakeley kid?"

"Roy? Surely I do. Everybody knows him."

"He's all wool and a yard wide, isn't he?"

"Yes, he's fine."

"Look out you don't trip on that rock.—He walked down the street with me last night and talked about—about that Slade fellow."

"Tom, you mean?"

"Yes; he's a staunch believer in Tom, even yet."

She made no answer.

"I think you kind of liked that fellow," said Roscoe teasingly.

"I always said if he ever made up his mind to do a thing he'd do it."

"Well, I guess he went and done it, as my old school grammar used to say."

"I don't like to hear you speak flippantly about him."

"How about me? Suppose I should make up my mind to do a thing—"

"Here we are at the bridge already," she said.

*　*　*　*　*

The new Y. M. C. A. Assembly Hall presented a gay scene, and they pushed through the crowd, Roscoe opening a way for the girl to pass, greeted on both hands by his friends and former companions. It seemed as if all the young people of the town were on hand; scouts were conspicuously in evidence, and among them all Mr. Ellsworth hustled genially about attending to a hundred and one duties.

"There you are," said Roscoe; "take that seat. Reminds you of that meeting on June fifth last when I wasn't with you—and Slade didn't show up either. Now, don't forget to clap when I stand up, will you?"

He swung up onto the platform, where Roy and Pee-wee and Doc Carson and Connie Bennett and the whole tribe of Silver Foxes clustered about him, helping him out of his big military coat and hovering about the chair he sat in. Even Dr. Wade, of the Y. M. C. A., and the gentlemen of the Local Scout Council received less attention.

As he sat there waiting, one or two of the scouts noticed (for scouts are nothing if not observant) that he craned his neck and looked far back into the lobby. If they thought twice about it, however, they probably attributed it to nervousness.

At last, after much impatient handclapping, all except the stage lights were dimmed, and Roy noticed again how the soldier peered searchingly into the back of the hall.

"Your mother and father coming?" he asked.

"They might stroll around."

"You look dandy," Roy whispered.

Roscoe grabbed him by the neck pleasantly and winked as he

Percy K. Fitzhugh

reached slyly over and pulled Pee-wee's belt axe from its martial sheath, to the amusement of some boys in the audience. But it was no matter for laughing, for if the Germans should break through the French lines at Verdun, say, and push through to Bordeaux, capture all the French transports, run the British blockade and make a sudden flank move against Bridgeboro, Pee-wee would be very thankful that he had his belt-axe along.

It was a great affair—that meeting. Dr. Wade told of the aims of the new Y. M. C. A.; the Methodist Scouts' gave an exhibition of pole jumping; the Elks (one member short) gave a demonstration of First-Aid bandaging, and a Red Cross woman gave a demonstration of surgery, for (as Roy said) she extracted *one bone* from everybody in the audience. Oh, it was a great affair! They had a movie play, *Scouts in Service*; the Bridgeboro Quartette sang *Over There*; a real, live Belgian refugee told how the gentle, kind Germans burned his little home and sent his sisters and brothers into slavery.

Perhaps it was this tragic story fresh in their minds which caused the crowd to clap vigorously when Private Bent, Second Infantry, U. S. A., jumped to his feet as Mr. Ellsworth finished introducing him and stood, feet close together, straight as an arrow, a little flush of embarrassment upon his handsome face, and threw his head back suddenly to get his little forelock of wavy hair out of the way.

It is no discredit to Dr. Wade or to Mr. Perry, of the Local Council, that Roscoe caught the audience with his first words. He was so young and fresh, so boyishly off-hand—so different from the others who had spoken. And then his straight young figure and his uniform!

"I don't know exactly why I'm here," he said; "I got this thing wished on me and you've got me wished on you. I'm sorry for you. So far as I'm concerned I guess I don't deserve any sympathy. I ran right into Scoutmaster Ellsworth with my eyes wide open [laughter] and he nabbed me. I should have kept my fingers crossed when I came back to Bridgeboro. He took me to his house and fed me on sugar—"

"You're lucky," some one called.

"And what could I do after that?"

"If I ever get clear of the Boy Scouts, believe me, I'll never get tangled up with them again. [Laughter.] But they tell me I'll see more of them in England and still more of them in France—so I guess there's no hope of getting away from them. [Laughter and applause.]

"If this thing keeps up we'll have to start a campaign to swat the scout, and see if we can't exterminate them in that way. [Uproarious shouts from Pee-wee.]

"But, ladies and gentlemen and scouts—not that scouts aren't gentlemen [laughter]—I don't think soldiers ought to be expected to make speeches. Actions speak louder than words, as the Kaiser will find out—[Pee-wee was restrained with difficulty.] So I'm just going to *do* something instead of standing here talking. Scoutmaster Ellsworth said for me to put plenty of pep into my little performance. And I'm going to put some tabasco sauce in it [Pee-wee again] and I hope it will hold him for a while.

"He introduced me as an enlisted soldier. Two thousand eight hundred and fifty-seven times in the last two days, he's called me that. It's a base libel! I didn't enlist; I was drafted. [Laughter.]

"And now I'm going to let you into a secret. Before Registration Day I felt pretty much as I felt about coming here to-night—I had cold feet. I have only the one thought now," he added, speaking more earnestly, "and that is to get over there and get one good whack at that crew of bandits and murderers! [Loud cheering.]

"But before Registration Day I was scared—just plain *scared*. You soon get rid of that when you get into the uniform. [Applause.] Well, I'm ashamed to say it, but I ran away. I had a crazy notion I could get away with it. I went up to a lonely place on a mountain near that big scout camp."

You could have heard a pin drop in the hall now.

"And one of these fellows—these scouts—suspected where I had gone and came up there after me and brought me to my senses." Roscoe's voice had grown gradually lower, and he spoke hesitatingly now, but the silence was so intense that every word was audible. "He pawned a gold medal he had to pay his way up there and he made me come back here. He missed his part in the big rally. He couldn't come back himself because he'd hurt his ankle.—He made me come back here where I belonged—to register!

"And then when he found—No, wait a minute, I'll read you the letter!"

He was in a fine frenzy of enthusiasm again now that he had finished the recital of his own shameful part in the affair. He took out Tom's letter and read it—read every word of it— and finished it with his cheeks flushed and his voice ringing:

"... so I'm going away to help in a way I can do without breaking my word to anybody. The thing I care most about is that you got registered. And next to that I'm glad because I like you"—Roscoe shook his head hastily and stopped for a second to control his voice—"because I like you and I always did—even when you made   fun of me—"

"What he liked me for, I'm hanged if I know—but that's the kind of a fellow Tom Slade is—"

"Whatever became of him?" some one on the platform whispered to some one else.

There was a slight sound back in the lobby of the hall.

"Somebody down there head him off; don't let him get away!" called Roscoe, stepping right to the front of the platform. "Start him down here! He didn't get away, did he?"

Roy Blakeley, vaulting over two rows of chairs, was in the aisle in three seconds. Everybody turned and looked toward the back of the hall. Some stood, peering cautiously into the dim lobby, where a little scuffle seemed to be going on. Then Roscoe himself leaped straight over the orchestra's space and started up the aisle.

But he was not needed. For Mr. Ellsworth himself had caught Tom by the collar, thrusting him out into the aisle, where Roy clutched aim by the arm.

And then the crowd saw him; saw him standing shame-facedly there as if still inclined to break away and run for it; his head hanging down, his big hand moving nervously on the old book-strap which he wore for a belt. The necktie, which presumably Mrs. O'Connor had furnished him, was all awry, and in the half light they could see, too, that his old clothes were faded and torn. He seemed quite indifferent to everybody and everything—even to Mr. Ellsworth—though

Percy K. Fitzhugh

he smiled nervously at Roscoe.

But Roy Blakeley, clinging to his arm, could feel what no one else could feel or see—Tom's hand pressing his wrist like a wireless signal, and Roy, like the bully scout he was, understood the code, took the message, and was silent.

CHAPTER XXVII

THE END OF THE TRAIL

Yes, that was a great meeting—it was a *peach* of a meeting!

"You broke your word," accused Tom, as Roscoe elbowed his way in.

"I did nothing of the kind. I asked you to trust a soldier's honor. You know more about a soldier's honor now than you did before, don't you?"

"*Good-night!*" laughed Roy. "No more soldier's honor for you! Hey, Tomasso? You've had enough of it."

Indeed he had had altogether too much of it. But his embarrassment passed as the bulk of the crowd, not involved in this surprising turn of affairs, took its way homeward, leaving the scouts and a few others in the hall. And soon things worked around so that Roscoe saw Tom alone. Not altogether alone, either, for Margaret Ellison was with him. How Roy and Pee-wee chanced to miss this I do not know.

The girl said very little, but stared at him until at last he said, "Are you looking at that scar? It don't look good, but it'll go away, I guess."

Percy K. Fitzhugh

"How did you get it?" she asked.

"He gave his place to another man," said Roscoe, "and was dumped into the ocean alone."

"A chunk of wood banged me in the forehead," said Tom simply.

"Tom, I want you to do me a favor,' said Roscoe, while Margaret continued to gaze at him. "It's a terribly impolite thing to suggest, but if you'd be willing to walk over to East Bridgeboro with Margaret, I could go home and get my things together. I'm afraid I'll miss the only train. You come to my house afterward and go to the train with me. You don't mind, do you, Marge? He'll protect you from the lions and tigers."

If she minded she didn't show it.

"I—ain't dressed up," said Tom awkwardly.

"I'm so glad of that!" she said.

*   *   *   *   *

Never in his life had he walked with a girl anywhere near his own age, and he felt just as he had felt that gala day when he had chatted with her in Temple Camp office. And because he was flustered and knew of nothing in particular to say, he repeated just what he had said then—that he could see she liked Roscoe, and he added that he didn't blame her, for Roscoe was "so good-looking in his uniform—kind of."

To this she made no answer; but after a few minutes she said, "Will you take me through Barrel Alley where you used to live?"

So Tom took her through Barrel Alley, answering her questions about his experiences and telling of spies and torpedoings and his rescue and cruise to South America simply, almost dully, as if they were things which were not worth talking about.

When they came behind John Temple's big bank building, they stood on the barrel staves whence the alley derived its name and counted the floors and picked out the windows of Temple Camp office.

"You'll come in and see Mr. Burton in the morning, won't you?" she said.

"Maybe," said Tom.

The good scout trail, which had wound over half the earth, took them on down that poor, sordid alley, and he showed her the tenement where he had once lived.

"The day we got put out," he said simply, "the sheriff stood a beer can on my mother's picture."

"Oh!" she said; "and then?"

"Nothing then," said Tom, "only I knocked him into the gutter. I got arrested."

They came out into the brighter light and clearer air of Main Street, and now the good scout trail, which indeed had not disappointed him, led them toward the quiet river and the willows and the hilly banks and across the bridge, from which he showed her the troop's cabin boat (soon to be plastered with Liberty Loan posters), and into the rural quiet of East Bridgeboro.

"I said it was a trail," said Tom.

"Yes?"

"I mean everything you do—kind of. It's just a trail. You don't know where it'll take you."

"It's just brought you back to the same place, hasn't it?" she said.

"But it won't stop," said Tom. "It don't make any difference, anyway, as long as you hit the right one. Once I thought it was kind of a crazy notion about everything you do being a trail. But now I know different. And if you do the wrong thing, you get on the wrong trail, that's all. Maybe you don't understand exactly what I mean."

"I do understand."

"It's brought me right back to where I'm talking to you again the same as on Registration Day. So you see it's a good trail. I got a kind of an idea that there can be a trail in your brain— like.—Often I think of things like that that I can't make other people understand—not even Roy sometimes.—I guess maybe girls understand better."

"Maybe," she said. "Do you see I'm wearing the little badge you gave me yet?"

They strolled on, following the trail, and neither spoke for a few minutes.

"In the end you don't get misjudged," said Tom simply, "because if you get on the right trail it'll bring you to the right place. If you've got the right on your side, you got to win."

"And that's why we'll win the war," she said.

"A feller that maybe got drowned told me about a little girl in London that got blown up while she was studying her lessons. And when I heard that I knew we'd win."

"Uncle Sam's like you, Tom," she laughed. "When he makes up his mind to do a thing.... Do you remember how you told me you had a good muscle? Uncle Sam's got a good muscle, don't you think?"

"I was thinking something like that when I looked at Roscoe to-night," he said. "We got to trust to Uncle Sam."

"The whole world is trusting to Uncle Sam now."

"He's got the muscle," said Tom.

"Yes."

The trail led through a fragrant avenue of evergreens now, through a solitude where Tom had often hiked, and presently they turned into the path which formed the short cut to the girl's home. Across the river, on the top of the bank building, they could see the Stars and Stripes waving in the small field of brightness thrown by the searchlight. And all else was darkness.

So, chatting idly, but all the while, coming to know each other better, they passed the log on which Tom and Roscoe had sat and talked, and strolled on through the dark, silent grove, where the lions and tigers were, and where the lonely screech-owl still hooted his dismal song.

Choose from Thousands of 1stWorldLibrary Classics By

A. M. Barnard
Ada Leverson
Adolphus William Ward
Aesop
Agatha Christie
Alexander Aaronsohn
Alexander Kielland
Alexandre Dumas
Alfred Gatty
Alfred Ollivant
Alice Duer Miller
Alice Turner Curtis
Alice Dunbar
Allen Chapman
Alleyne Ireland
Ambrose Bierce
Amelia E. Barr
Amory H. Bradford
Andrew Lang
Andrew McFarland Davis
Andy Adams
Angela Brazil
Anna Alice Chapin
Anna Sewell
Annie Besant
Annie Hamilton Donnell
Annie Payson Call
Annie Roe Carr
Annonaymous
Anton Chekhov
Archibald Lee Fletcher
Arnold Bennett
Arthur C. Benson
Arthur Conan Doyle
Arthur M. Winfield
Arthur Ransome
Arthur Schnitzler
Arthur Train
Atticus
B.H. Baden-Powell
B. M. Bower
B. C. Chatterjee
Baroness Emmuska Orczy
Baroness Orczy
Basil King
Bayard Taylor
Ben Macomber
Bertha Muzzy Bower
Bjornstjerne Bjornson

Booth Tarkington
Boyd Cable
Bram Stoker
C. Collodi
C. E. Orr
C. M. Ingleby
Carolyn Wells
Catherine Parr Traill
Charles A. Eastman
Charles Amory Beach
Charles Dickens
Charles Dudley Warner
Charles Farrar Browne
Charles Ives
Charles Kingsley
Charles Klein
Charles Hanson Towne
Charles Lathrop Pack
Charles Romyn Dake
Charles Whibley
Charles Willing Beale
Charlotte M. Braeme
Charlotte M. Yonge
Charlotte Perkins Stetson
Clair W. Hayes
Clarence Day Jr.
Clarence E. Mulford
Clemence Housman
Confucius
Coningsby Dawson
Cornelis DeWitt Wilcox
Cyril Burleigh
D. H. Lawrence
Daniel Defoe
David Garnett
Dinah Craik
Don Carlos Janes
Donald Keyhoe
Dorothy Kilner
Dougan Clark
Douglas Fairbanks
E. Nesbit
E. P. Roe
E. Phillips Oppenheim
E. S. Brooks
Earl Barnes
Edgar Rice Burroughs
Edith Van Dyne
Edith Wharton

Edward Everett Hale
Edward J. O'Biren
Edward S. Ellis
Edwin L. Arnold
Eleanor Atkins
Eleanor Hallowell Abbott
Eliot Gregory
Elizabeth Gaskell
Elizabeth McCracken
Elizabeth Von Arnim
Ellem Key
Emerson Hough
Emilie F. Carlen
Emily Bronte
Emily Dickinson
Enid Bagnold
Enilor Macartney Lane
Erasmus W. Jones
Ernie Howard Pie
Ethel May Dell
Ethel Turner
Ethel Watts Mumford
Eugene Sue
Eugenie Foa
Eugene Wood
Eustace Hale Ball
Evelyn Everett-green
Everard Cotes
F. H. Cheley
F. J. Cross
F. Marion Crawford
Fannie E. Newberry
Federick Austin Ogg
Ferdinand Ossendowski
Fergus Hume
Florence A. Kilpatrick
Fremont B. Deering
Francis Bacon
Francis Darwin
Frances Hodgson Burnett
Frances Parkinson Keyes
Frank Gee Patchin
Frank Harris
Frank Jewett Mather
Frank L. Packard
Frank V. Webster
Frederic Stewart Isham
Frederick Trevor Hill
Frederick Winslow Taylor

Friedrich Kerst
Friedrich Nietzsche
Fyodor Dostoyevsky
G.A. Henty
G.K. Chesterton
Gabrielle E. Jackson
Garrett P. Serviss
Gaston Leroux
George A. Warren
George Ade
Geroge Bernard Shaw
George Cary Eggleston
George Durston
George Ebers
George Eliot
George Gissing
George MacDonald
George Meredith
George Orwell
George Sylvester Viereck
George Tucker
George W. Cable
George Wharton James
Gertrude Atherton
Gordon Casserly
Grace E. King
Grace Gallatin
Grace Greenwood
Grant Allen
Guillermo A. Sherwell
Gulielma Zollinger
Gustav Flaubert
H. A. Cody
H. B. Irving
H.C. Bailey
H. G. Wells
H. H. Munro
H. Irving Hancock
H. R. Naylor
H. Rider Haggard
H. W. C. Davis
Haldeman Julius
Hall Caine
Hamilton Wright Mabie
Hans Christian Andersen
Harold Avery
Harold McGrath
Harriet Beecher Stowe
Harry Castlemon
Harry Coghill
Harry Houidini

Hayden Carruth
Helent Hunt Jackson
Helen Nicolay
Hendrik Conscience
Hendy David Thoreau
Henri Barbusse
Henrik Ibsen
Henry Adams
Henry Ford
Henry Frost
Henry James
Henry Jones Ford
Henry Seton Merriman
Henry W Longfellow
Herbert A. Giles
Herbert Carter
Herbert N. Casson
Herman Hesse
Hildegard G. Frey
Homer
Honore De Balzac
Horace B. Day
Horace Walpole
Horatio Alger Jr.
Howard Pyle
Howard R. Garis
Hugh Lofting
Hugh Walpole
Humphry Ward
Ian Maclaren
Inez Haynes Gillmore
Irving Bacheller
Isabel Cecilia Williams
Isabel Hornibrook
Israel Abrahams
Ivan Turgenev
J.G.Austin
J. Henri Fabre
J. M. Barrie
J. M. Walsh
J. Macdonald Oxley
J. R. Miller
J. S. Fletcher
J. S. Knowles
J. Storer Clouston
J. W. Duffield
Jack London
Jacob Abbott
James Allen
James Andrews
James Baldwin

James Branch Cabell
James DeMille
James Joyce
James Lane Allen
James Lane Allen
James Oliver Curwood
James Oppenheim
James Otis
James R. Driscoll
Jane Abbott
Jane Austen
Jane L. Stewart
Janet Aldridge
Jens Peter Jacobsen
Jerome K. Jerome
Jessie Graham Flower
John Buchan
John Burroughs
John Cournos
John F. Kennedy
John Gay
John Glasworthy
John Habberton
John Joy Bell
John Kendrick Bangs
John Milton
John Philip Sousa
John Taintor Foote
Jonas Lauritz Idemil Lie
Jonathan Swift
Joseph A. Altsheler
Joseph Carey
Joseph Conrad
Joseph E. Badger Jr
Joseph Hergesheimer
Joseph Jacobs
Jules Vernes
Julian Hawthrone
Julie A Lippmann
Justin Huntly McCarthy
Kakuzo Okakura
Karle Wilson Baker
Kate Chopin
Kenneth Grahame
Kenneth McGaffey
Kate Langley Bosher
Kate Langley Bosher
Katherine Cecil Thurston
Katherine Stokes
L. A. Abbot
L. T. Meade

L. Frank Baum
Latta Griswold
Laura Dent Crane
Laura Lee Hope
Laurence Housman
Lawrence Beasley
Leo Tolstoy
Leonid Andreyev
Lewis Carroll
Lewis Sperry Chafer
Lilian Bell
Lloyd Osbourne
Louis Hughes
Louis Joseph Vance
Louis Tracy
Louisa May Alcott
Lucy Fitch Perkins
Lucy Maud Montgomery
Luther Benson
Lydia Miller Middleton
Lyndon Orr
M. Corvus
M. H. Adams
Margaret E. Sangster
Margret Howth
Margaret Vandercook
Margaret W. Hungerford
Margret Penrose
Maria Edgeworth
Maria Thompson Daviess
Mariano Azuela
Marion Polk Angellotti
Mark Overton
Mark Twain
Mary Austin
Mary Catherine Crowley
Mary Cole
Mary Hastings Bradley
Mary Roberts Rinehart
Mary Rowlandson
M. Wollstonecraft Shelley
Maud Lindsay
Max Beerbohm
Myra Kelly
Nathaniel Hawthrone
Nicolo Machiavelli
O. F. Walton
Oscar Wilde

Owen Johnson
P.G. Wodehouse
Paul and Mabel Thorne
Paul G. Tomlinson
Paul Severing
Percy Brebner
Percy Keese Fitzhugh
Peter B. Kyne
Plato
Quincy Allen
R. Derby Holmes
R. L. Stevenson
R. S. Ball
Rabindranath Tagore
Rahul Alvares
Ralph Bonehill
Ralph Henry Barbour
Ralph Victor
Ralph Waldo Emmerson
Rene Descartes
Ray Cummings
Rex Beach
Rex E. Beach
Richard Harding Davis
Richard Jefferies
Richard Le Gallienne
Robert Barr
Robert Frost
Robert Gordon Anderson
Robert L. Drake
Robert Lansing
Robert Lynd
Robert Michael Ballantyne
Robert W. Chambers
Rosa Nouchette Carey
Rudyard Kipling
Saint Augustine
Samuel B. Allison
Samuel Hopkins Adams
Sarah Bernhardt
Sarah C. Hallowell
Selma Lagerlof
Sherwood Anderson
Sigmund Freud
Standish O'Grady
Stanley Weyman
Stella Benson
Stella M. Francis

Stephen Crane
Stewart Edward White
Stijn Streuvels
Swami Abhedananda
Swami Parmananda
T. S. Ackland
T. S. Arthur
The Princess Der Ling
Thomas A. Janvier
Thomas A Kempis
Thomas Anderton
Thomas Bailey Aldrich
Thomas Bulfinch
Thomas De Quincey
Thomas Dixon
Thomas H. Huxley
Thomas Hardy
Thomas More
Thornton W. Burgess
U. S. Grant
Upton Sinclair
Valentine Williams
Various Authors
Vaughan Kester
Victor Appleton
Victor G. Durham
Victoria Cross
Virginia Woolf
Wadsworth Camp
Walter Camp
Walter Scott
Washington Irving
Wilbur Lawton
Wilkie Collins
Willa Cather
Willard F. Baker
William Dean Howells
William le Queux
W. Makepeace Thackeray
William W. Walter
William Shakespeare
Winston Churchill
Yei Theodora Ozaki
Yogi Ramacharaka
Young E. Allison
Zane Grey